MW01094157

The New Black Middle Class
in the Twenty-First Century

The New Black Middle Class in the Twenty-First Century

~

BART LANDRY

Rutgers University Press

New Brunswick, Camden, and Newark, New Jersey, and London

The New Black Middle Class in the Twenty-First Century,
Library of Congress Cataloging in Publication Number: 2017055379

A British Cataloging-in-Publication record for this book is available
from the British Library.

∞ The paper used in this publication meets the requirements of the American
National Standard for Information Sciences—Permanence of Paper for Printed
Library Materials, ANSI Z39.48-1992.

www.rutgersuniversitypress.org

Manufactured in the United States of America

For my wife, Rita,
and for
Cyan, Ethan, Evan, and Isabella

Contents

The New Black Middle Class
in the Twenty-First Century

Introduction

It has been thirty years since I published *The New Black Middle Class*, in which I distinguished between an "old black middle class" and a "new black middle class."[1] The former had risen in a segregated era to serve the unmet needs of the black community in health care, education, and law. The latter emerged only after passage of the 1964 Civil Rights Act, which banned discrimination in education and the labor force. With access to all colleges and universities, black graduates could enter a broader range of professional, managerial, and other white-collar occupations, creating a new black middle class. It was a new black middle class also because its members now had access to previously barred institutions of society: restaurants, parks, beaches, hotels, and transportation. While there had been discrimination in the North before 1964, it was especially in the South, where most blacks still lived, that the civil rights legislation had its greatest and most visible impact. College-educated middle-class blacks no longer faced the indignities of having to use "Colored Only" bathrooms, water fountains, and buses. Implementation of the law was sometimes slow, as when I was directed to a "Colored Only" bathroom during a stop for gas at a small town in Georgia in 1966. Nevertheless, change had come to the South, and the black middle class now lived in a new environment with greatly improved life chances. For the most part, they could spend their money where and how they pleased.

In defining the black middle class I follow the approach of Max Weber, who thought of class in terms of position in the economy.[2] The upper class, according to Weber, is composed of those who own property, which today includes large industrial and service corporations, major financial institutions such as banks and equity funds, as well as extensive real estate holdings. Members of the other classes achieve their position when they enter the labor market. Those with nonmanual skills (education) form the white-collar middle class; those with manual skills form the working class. In distinguishing between those who own property and those who do not, Weber agreed with Karl Marx's class model of bourgeoisie and proletariat.[3] Their agreement ended there, however. Writing at a time in the early twentieth century when corporations were creating large numbers of white-collar jobs, Weber recognized the emergence of a new class, one that occupied a place between the bourgeoisie and the proletariat. One can further distinguish between an upper middle class of professionals and administrators/executives and a lower middle class of workers in technical, sales, and clerical positions. From Weber's perspective, the compensation (salary and benefits) attached to jobs in the labor market determines one's standard of living. The newly created "middle class" was distinguished by its higher compensation—in comparison with that of manual workers' compensations—which translated into a superior standard of living.

One sometimes encounters articles announcing the "decline of the middle class." The authors are typically economists who use income categories (quintiles) rather than occupation to define class. Incomes, they note, have declined or stagnated for many white-collar workers. This may erode living standards but does not mean that those individuals have dropped out of the middle class. An engineer with a lower or stagnant salary is still an engineer. Membership in a class is dependent on ownership or occupation, not level of income.

The emergence of a new black middle class was not without its challenges. Change, especially radical change in society, rarely unfolds smoothly. Sensitivity to this fact led Congress to create the

Equal Employment Opportunity Commission (EEOC) in 1965 to administer and enforce the new law against employment discrimination. The EEOC was a place where individuals could go for redress in cases of discrimination in hiring and disparate treatment in compensation and promotion. With a greatly enlarged mandate beyond discrimination in the workplace, the commission continues to this day.

The New Black Middle Class appeared when academic scholars and policy experts were still primarily focused on the black poor. To some extent, this was understandable. In 1970, only 13 percent of employed blacks held middle-class jobs, up from only 10 percent in 1960. Poverty research had become an academic cottage industry that produced a voluminous literature on every aspect of poverty. These studies inadvertently helped stigmatize blacks as a community of poor people rather than one with a class hierarchy similar to that of whites. I wrote *The New Black Middle Class* to dispel this stereotype. Although small, there was a black middle class composed of an upper stratum of professionals and administrators and a lower stratum of technical, sales, and clerical white-collar workers. There was also a large working class. The relative proportions of blacks and whites in each class differed markedly (more whites in the middle class and more blacks in the working class); yet African Americans did have a class structure similar to whites. Equally important—and not surprising given the historical experiences of blacks—I found great disparities in educational, occupational, income, and wealth attainment between the black and white middle classes. Still, *The New Black Middle Class* firmly established the existence of a black middle class in the United States. This new black middle class has continued to grow over the decades. Following the Weberian approach in defining class by occupation, the black and white middle classes, composed of white-collar workers (professionals, executives/administrators, and technical, clerical, and sales workers) were approximately 52 and 63 percent of their respective labor forces in 2010 (see Appendix).[4] The middle class is divided into upper and lower strata, with the upper middle class composed of professionals and executives/

administrators; while technical, clerical, and sales workers form the lower middle class. The gap between the black and white upper middle classes has remained roughly the same, as both have grown significantly since 1983.

The New Black Middle Class was not the first book on the black middle class, but it was the first to use national representative data. E. Franklin Frazier's *Black Bourgeoisie*, published in 1957, was an important book that raised many questions about the black middle class.[5] Its use of anecdotal material, however, failed to provide solid answers to the questions raised. Other studies followed *The New Black Middle Class*. Prominent among these studies have been Joe R. Feagin and Melvin P. Sikes's *Living with Racism: The Black Middle-Class Experience* (1994), Sharon Collins's *Black Corporate Executives: The Making and Breaking of a Black Middle Class* (1997), Mary Pattillo-McCoy's *Black Picket Fences: Privilege and Peril among the Black Middle Class* (1999), and Karyn R. Lacy's *Blue-Chip Black: Race, Class, and Status in the New Black Middle Class* (2007).[6] The literature on the black middle class has also included a large outpouring of scholarly articles on a variety of topics that my colleague Kris Marsh and I analyzed in our article "The Evolution of the New Black Middle Class," published in the *Annual Review of Sociology* in 2011.[7] We examined approximately ninety-four books and articles, which were divided into thirteen topics covering both historical and contemporary issues.

In the mid-2000s, I began thinking of a new study of the black middle class that would examine the changes that had occurred since publication of my book. This endeavor became *The New Black Middle Class in the Twenty-First Century*. I use both qualitative and quantitative data, an approach known in sociology as a mixed-method approach. Qualitative and quantitative studies have strengths and weaknesses. Quantitative studies use representative samples that allow one to generalize to larger populations but often lack in-depth insights that can only come from qualitative data. While qualitative data lack statistical generalizability, they provide a more nuanced and in-depth understanding of the subject. Combining both approaches in the same study maximizes the strengths of both while minimizing their weaknesses.

For quantitative data, I relied on various U.S. Census surveys. This allowed me to trace changes in topics such as education over fifty years and to compare the educational achievements of blacks with those of whites. The qualitative data come from thirty-one face-to-face interviews with upper-middle-class African American families in Prince George's County, Maryland, which is located in the Washington, D.C., metropolitan area. I interviewed both spouses. I should note that most of these couples are from the professional stratum of the upper middle class, although some of them were also managers and supervisors at different times in their careers. In this sense my sample does not include members of the black lower middle class (sales, technical, and clerical white-collar workers). This was done partly for time and resource reasons but also because upper-middle-class occupations form the class stratum that is most often thought of when we speak of the middle class in the United States. These occupations are also the aspirational destination of the upwardly mobile, the mark of success. Studying these occupations is a test of the degree of success that African Americans have achieved in the twenty-first century.

As was the case of *The New Black Middle Class*, the goal of this study is to present a comprehensive picture of new black middle-class life today, in the twenty-first century. I tried to anticipate questions someone might have when hearing that there is a black middle class. In the face of the vulgar level of economic inequality in the United States today, recently protested by the Occupy Wall Street movement, some might wonder about the income and wealth achievement of the members of today's new black middle class. It is a topic that a number of scholars have investigated.[8] Each has added something to our understanding of racial economic inequality. Wealth research, however, is plagued by a number of difficulties, including varying definitions of "middle class," different measurements, and the tendency to compare all blacks with all whites. My approach, although not completely unique, focuses on the different components of wealth, with multiple comparisons across middle-class blacks and whites rather than all blacks and all whites.

Others may want to know about the bedrock issues of educational and occupational attainment, the sources of an individual's living standard. In the United States, one's life ambience, where one lives, is also part of an individual's or family's living standard. An upscale home in a quiet suburban neighborhood is the image most people associate with life in the middle class. Residential location is also an area that has historically been fraught with racial tension, exclusion, and violence. How members of the new black middle class are navigating this area today is an important part of this study. I explore their aspirations and achievements in finding "places of their own."[9] In spite of the long history focused on residential integration, the answers I found may be surprising to many. The middle class grows through upward mobility or "inheritance" of parents' middle-class position. This does not occur by chance. I explore in depth the efforts of these families to ensure their children follow in their footsteps.

Throughout this book I give prominence to the voices of the interviewed couples rather than merely summarizing their responses. With the qualitative data, I use the interviewees' own voices to tell the story of the new black middle class in the twenty-first century. I provide analytic frameworks and interpretations, where necessary, but I allow the interviewees to tell the stories of their lives. The quantitative data provide the historical and national settings for these narratives. It is my hope that this approach will offer lively reading as well as accuracy and authenticity. I end with an Afterword that fills some of the gaps since the couples were interviewed.

1

The New Black Middle Class and the Demographics of the Twenty-First Century

Place has always loomed large in African American history, beginning with the forceful removal of Africans from a place of their own to a place of chattel slavery in the United States, the Caribbean, and South America. The search for a place of their own continued in the post-emancipation period and accelerated in the twentieth century with the Great Migration of black individuals and families to urban manufacturing centers of the North and Midwest. In *Places of Their Own*, Andrew Wiese traces this migration to the suburbs of major metropolitan areas.[1]

This movement to suburban communities did not come early. Although new modes of transportation facilitated migration from manufacturing cities to suburban areas in the late nineteenth century (for example, Manhattan to Brooklyn) and early twentieth century, the pace was slow and dominated by whites. Not until the post–World War II period did the American romance with suburban living become part of the American Dream. Suburbs were spacious, clean, and white; a good place to raise children. New federal loan programs (through the Federal Housing Administration and the GI Bill) provided guarantees to banks for home loans and helped lenders introduce the thirty-year mortgage. The cookie-cutter homes of the Levittowns (New York,

1947–1951, and Pennsylvania, 1952–1958) created new communities in wide-open spaces. President Eisenhower's highway program and Detroit automobiles provided the incentives and means to flee deteriorating city centers. There was, however, one flaw in this scenario: blacks could not participate in this city-to-suburb movement of the 1950s and 1960s. A system of "redlining" shut out black families from bank mortgages in racially mixed or black suburban communities.

Recent changes in the demography of the U.S. population have increased interest in the racial and ethnic composition of communities in both the cities and suburbs of major metropolitan areas. Diversity and segregation dominate this research, and new terminology introduced into these discussions strains to capture the novelty and complexity of recent and contemporary changes. Many cities and suburbs have become "melting pots" because of the diversity of their populations, including Asians, African Americans, Latinos, and whites. While whites dominated the early suburbanization movement, it is Asians, African Americans, and Latinos who now lead the migration to suburbs today, according to demographer William Frey.[2] There are two ways to look at these suburban population shifts: as a group's share of the total suburban population in these major metro areas or as the percentage of a group's *own* metropolitan population that resides in the suburbs. The first reveals modest increases over the past three decades. Between 1990 and 2010, blacks increased their share of the suburban population from 7 to 10 percent, Asians from 3 to 6 percent, and Latinos from 8 to 17 percent. Although each group's increase appears modest, nationally their combined shares rose to 35 percent of the suburban population of the one hundred largest metros, as the white percentage shrank from 81 to 65 percent.

Statistics of a group's city-to-suburb migration yield more interesting findings. Nationwide, the percentage of blacks living in the suburbs of the one hundred largest metropolitan areas increased from 37 percent in 1990 to 51 percent in 2010. Their highest concentrations, according to Frey's analysis, were in the southern metros of New Orleans, Louisiana; Jackson, Mississippi; Memphis, Tennessee; Atlanta, Georgia; Columbia, South Carolina; Charleston, South Carolina; Richmond, Virginia; and Virginia Beach, Virginia. Collectively, these cities had black suburban populations between 35 and 50 percent in 2010. The Washington, D.C., metro stood out with 51 percent of its black population living in its suburbs. With the exception of Miami, Chicago, New York, and Honolulu, Latinos and Asians, in contrast to African Americans, realized their highest level of suburbanization in the western states of California, Arizona, New Mexico, and Texas. Significant concentrations of suburban minorities are now in southern and western states. Among the southern and border metros, four led the way with the highest percentage of black suburbanites: Atlanta, Dallas, Houston, and Washington, D.C. These racial and ethnic migrations in the one hundred major metropolitan areas have changed the demography of suburban America, often from places of white residential communities to what Frey calls "melting-pot" suburbs: suburbs where at least 35 percent of residents are nonwhite. Melting-pot suburbs include thirty-six of the one hundred largest metro areas. Among these thirty-six, sixteen were *majority-minority* suburbs in 2010.[3] The high rate of recent black movement to suburbs prompted Frey to write of a "breakthrough black flight" from cities with large black populations. Today a higher percentage of blacks, Asians, and Latinos in large metro areas live in suburbs than in central cities.

The increasing diversity of suburbs in the major metropolitan areas forecasts significant social, economic, and political changes. Suburban living has brought the American Dream closer to many minority groups and has become preferable to the inner-city spaces that nonwhites have historically occupied. Yet not all suburban residents have gained equally. We have only to think of Ferguson, Missouri, to realize that poverty has taken root in many of these suburbs. At times it is the result of "spillover" suburbanization: the migration of poor individuals and families from contiguous poverty areas in metropolitan cities. The reason for this migration may be a search for perceived safer and more organized communities or the push factor of rising rents.

Several scholars have researched rates of segregation and poverty in the suburbs of major metropolitan areas. Myron Orfield and Thomas Luce identify four types of suburbs among the 50 fifty largest metropolitan areas: (1) diverse, (2) mainly nonwhite, (3) mostly white, and (4) exurbs.[4] Diverse suburbs are those with 20 to 60 percent nonwhite residents; mainly nonwhite suburbs have over 60 percent nonwhite residents; mostly white suburbs are more than 80 percent white; and exurbs, sometimes referred to as "outer suburbs" or "exurbia," are less than 10 percent urban and predominantly white. Economic well-being, education, and governmental services vary across these four types of suburbs.

White suburbs have the best educational systems, the lowest poverty rates, and the best community services. Diverse suburbs rank second in these areas, while nonwhite suburbs often suffer from poor-performing schools, poor services, and high levels of poverty. With 44 percent of the total suburban population (53 million people) in 1,376 suburbs (up from 42 million in 1,006 suburbs in 2000), diverse suburbs represented the largest category of suburbs in the fifty largest metro areas in 2010, according to Orfield and Luce. Second in number of inhabitants were the largely white suburbs with 47 million residents, or 28 percent of suburban dwellers—down from 35 percent (54 million)—in 2000. Nonwhite suburbs ranked third, with 17 percent (20 million) of suburbanites in 478 suburbs. This was an increase of 12 percent from 2000.

Diverse, integrated suburbs are viewed by some scholars as the ideal type and the country's best hope for progress beyond inequality and our segregated past. Orfield and Luce argue, "Integrated [diverse] communities have the greatest success eliminating racial disparities in education and economic opportunity."[5] Yet they note the vulnerability of these communities; diverse, integrated suburban communities are difficult to maintain over long periods. They found that suburban neighborhoods with over 23 percent nonwhite residents in 1980 "were more likely to be predominantly nonwhite (over 60%) by 2005 than to remain integrated."[6]

John Logan, a sociologist at Brown University, points to another troubling characteristic of black suburban neighborhoods in 2010: higher poverty rates than those with mostly white residents. His research found that although exposure to poverty declines as black incomes rise, those with incomes above $75,000 lived in suburban communities with a higher poverty rate (9 percent) than whites with incomes below $40,000 (8.2 percent).[7] Logan also found that "suburban residents are divided by racial/ethnic boundaries" and that "blacks and Hispanics live in the least desirable neighborhoods, even when they can afford better."[8]

Research on the one hundred or fifty largest metropolitan areas of the United States has revealed major population shifts since the 1960s and 1970s. Suburbs are no longer synonymous with white residency and central cities with black residency. Increased Latino immigration and significant African American and Asian migration to the suburbs of the largest metropolitan areas have created a new, unfolding reality that has brought both new opportunities and challenges. For African Americans, this suburbanization process has progressed fastest in southern and border metropolitan areas, with four cities—Atlanta, Dallas, Houston, and Washington, D.C.—leading the trend. Among these four, the Washington, D.C., metropolitan area ranks highest, with 51 percent of its black residents living in suburbs.

When I published *The New Black Middle Class* in 1987, I did not address this issue since the level of black suburbanization was still minuscule. Today there is a need to assess these changes as they affect the lives of the new black middle class in these suburbs. To accomplish this, I conducted in-depth, face-to-face interviews with thirty-one couples in Prince George's County, Maryland, the county with the highest concentration of middle-class black suburbanites in the Washington, D.C., metropolitan area. Understanding black middle-class suburbanization in Prince George's County not only provides insights into new black middle-class suburban life in the Washington, D.C., metro but also a better understanding of the growing black middle-class suburbanization in other major metros.

There are differences among black middle-class suburbanites across metropolitan areas, but all share to some extent in a black culture with deep roots in the South. A high percentage of blacks in the D.C. metropolitan area migrated from southern states or are the children of southern migrants. As we will see, many of Prince George's middle-class blacks attended historically black colleges and universities (HBCUs) in the South before returning to the Washington, D.C., metro. The four leading metropolitan areas (Atlanta, Dallas, Houston, and Washington, D.C.) all provide fertile ground for developing large black middle-class suburban communities. Three (D.C., Atlanta, and Houston) already had large metropolitan populations of over four million in 1990, with Dallas close behind with 3.5 million. Each also had a large base of African Americans, ranging from almost one million to nearly two million in 2010. The education levels of their black populations were, with a few exceptions, also far higher than in smaller metros like Memphis and Charleston. As we will see later, this is important for the growth of black middle-class suburbs since over half of black college graduates live in suburbs. In 2000, Washington, D.C.'s black suburbanites led with 30.8 percent college graduates, followed closely by Atlanta (25.6 percent), Dallas (25.3 percent), and Houston (23 percent). Large metros and black populations with high levels of education appear to provide fertile ground for the growth of the largest black middle-class suburbs. There are, however, large metropolitan areas like Chicago and Philadelphia with large black populations that have not developed middle-class black suburbs as large as the four above. Lower levels of black college graduates in their suburbs (21.7 percent and 21.9 percent in the Chicago and Philadelphia metro areas) seem to be an important factor.

Beyond the important similarities shared by the four metros with the largest black middle-class suburbs, there are differences that might explain why Washington, D.C., and Atlanta are the leaders among the four. Blacks and whites in the Washington, D.C., metropolitan area have the highest education level among major metro areas, in part because of the large number of excellent universities in the area and in part because its service economy and federal bureaucracy draw college graduates. The federal government has had a very strong economic impact through its direct and indirect contributions to a knowledge economy. Because of the historically black Howard University and early access to government employment through civil service exams, a large black middle class developed earlier here than in other major metropolitan areas. The Atlanta metro comes closest to the experience of blacks in the Washington, D.C., metro because of a cluster of HBCUs there and a large African American population. Dallas and Houston follow closely in the sizes of both their overall metropolitan and their black populations, but until recently they have lacked similar educational resources to grow large black middle classes. Of the smaller metropolitan areas that Frey cites, Columbia (24 percent), Memphis (20.8 percent), and Richmond (19.6 percent) come closest to the percentages of black suburbanites with college degrees found in the four leading metros in 2000. The overall and black populations in these three metros are much smaller than in the largest metros. In 2010, Memphis had 1.3 million overall metro population and 601,043 blacks, Richmond 1.2 million metro population and 375,427 blacks, and Columbia 767,598 overall population and 255,102 blacks. Although individually small, together these southern middle-class suburbs also contribute to the growth in the number of black middle-class suburbanites.

Middle-class blacks in the Washington, D.C., suburb of Prince George's County represent middle-class blacks in the other large and small metropolitan area suburbs. In the following chapters, I explore various aspects of their lives in the county, beginning with their settlement there, continuing with social and economic aspects of their lives, and ending with their efforts to prepare the next generation of middle-class African Americans.

2

Suburbanization of the New Black Middle Class

Each of the eleven metropolitan areas with the highest concentrations of black suburbanites (Atlanta, Dallas, Houston, Washington, D.C., New Orleans, Jackson, Memphis, Columbia, Charleston, Richmond, and Virginia Beach) is part of the recent trend of minority migration from city to suburb. They form a new chapter in the lives of nonwhites who were shut out of the earlier city-to-suburb migration of the post–World War II era. For African Americans, who have the longest history of residence in the United States after Native Americans and white immigrants, this has been an especially important development. It represents a significant victory in the long struggle to exercise the important right to choose one's residential location. While there are still barriers in the migration of minority groups, some of the most difficult ones have been either weakened or eliminated. This is especially true of dismantled discriminatory housing laws and illegal restrictive covenants against the sale of homes to African Americans and Jews.

Of the eleven metropolitan areas with the highest black middle-class suburban concentration, Washington, D.C., is located the farthest north. Like the other ten areas, black suburbanization has been facilitated by population size and college attainment. Washington, D.C., had the additional factor of a large federal bureaucracy with a civil service hiring system that blacks were able to access. Still, Washington, D.C., and the surrounding counties have been part of the residential segregated system of the South that barred even upper-middle-class blacks from migrating to the suburbs. The development of middle-class black suburbs in the Washington, D.C., metropolitan area, therefore, is part of the story of middle-class suburbanization in all eleven suburbs.

The District of Columbia is surrounded by the counties of Maryland and Virginia. Middle-class blacks have migrated to all of these counties but in different numbers. The largest numbers have settled in Prince George's County, Maryland. Why did this happen in a county noted for its history of slavery and slave markets? The state of Maryland, while not part of the Deep South, is a border state that shares some of the Deep South's slavery experience—with a unique twist. Unlike the states of the Deep South, nineteenth-century Maryland was home to both slave and free blacks. The state's economy—divided along a north-south axis, one part agricultural, the other more industrial—and its proximity to the nonslave North may have contributed to its uniqueness. By the middle of the nineteenth century, the northern counties of the state, including the city of Baltimore, had a diversified economy that included manufacturing and depended on a mixed labor force of whites and both free and slave blacks. Southern counties, including Prince George's County, remained committed to cotton cultivation using slave labor. As the northern region of the state grew in economic strength and population, the southern half took defensive measures to preserve its slave labor force. In the new state constitution of 1851, slaveholders included a provision that prevented the legislature from abolishing slavery.

This and other proslavery efforts of the southern counties could not stem the tide of change in the state. The increasing disinterest of Baltimore and other northern counties in maintaining slave labor and the ever-growing free black population (even in southern parts of the state) weakened slavery in Maryland to an extent not possible in the Deep South. By the mid-nineteenth century, Prince George's County increasingly mirrored the state's north-south split. Its geographic position between Baltimore and Washington encouraged economic diversification from tobacco to agricultural products that could serve the growing markets of Baltimore and Washington, D.C. By 1850, according to historian Ira Berlin,[1] whites and free blacks made up 47 percent of Prince George's population, with slaves making up the rest. Even with these changes, Prince George's and the other southern counties remained mired in a failing economic model and a declining population. The antislavery movement and the Civil War would soon come to the state and lead to its official abolishment of slavery in 1864. This did not result in the incorporation of free and freed blacks into the civic community of the state. Like southern states, Maryland would resort to segregation as a tool for continued subjugation of its black population. Like the rest of southern Maryland, Prince George's County would remain a sleepy, mostly white, rural, segregated county, until overtaken by the upheavals of the civil rights movement in the mid-1960s. As we will see below, disputes over school desegregation soon followed these struggles in the late 1960s.

Fast-forward to a 1992 article by David Dent entitled "The New Black Suburbs" in which he described the growing black upper middle class in the Mitchellville suburb of Prince George's County.[2] The article, published in the prestigious *New York Times Magazine*, called attention to a process that had been under way for several decades. How did this happen in this former slave state rather than in a suburb of a northern city such as Philadelphia, New York, or Boston?

The Making of the Largest Black Middle-Class Suburb

Given the county's historical past, why have so many upper-middle-class blacks chosen to make it their home? In 1970, Prince George's County was still rural and agricultural, with a black population that had shrunk to only 13.9 percent. Most blacks had migrated since the late nineteenth century to the more prosperous and liberal areas of Baltimore and Washington, D.C. The late 1960s and early '70s was also a period of intense struggle over school desegregation between Prince George's school board and the federal government that ended with a judgment of noncompliance in 1971. A judicial order mandating busing for school desegregation followed the noncompliance judgment in the largest school system so affected in the country. Prince George's County had entered a period of intense conflict over school desegregation that would lead to significant demographic changes. Discussions centered on the future character of the county. Would it remain a predominantly white suburb, become integrated, or tip into the nonwhite column as others had done? Over the coming decades, intense interest focused on the possibility that the county would be an example of a stable integrated community, a melting-pot suburb. The question remained, however: Why did upper-middle-class blacks move into a county suffering from the upheavals of school desegregation and an acknowledged underperforming school system? Why did they not choose one of the more developed surrounding counties, such as Montgomery County or Fairfax County in Virginia?

By 1980, the black population of Prince George's County had grown to 37 percent. What motivated this migration to the county? I sought to answer this question through face-to-face interviews with thirty-one upper-middle-class black couples who lived in the county in 2007. Given the 1992 article by David Dent on the county's growing black middle class, I expected to hear stories of how the cachet of an affluent black middle-class community had drawn them to move there. I soon discovered that the development of this black middle-class suburban community was far more complex than I had imagined. In part, it is the quintessential story of Americans who move an average of 11.7 times in search of a better life. As it unfolded, I learned of the twists and turns of the African American version of this story line.

Analysis of the thirty-one interviews revealed that these families entered the county over a period of twenty-three years, from

1979 to 2004. During this period, the demography of Prince George's County changed radically, from 37 percent black in 1980 to about 63 percent black by 2004. The couples interviewed fell into three groups: nine families that moved into the county in the 1980s (with one exception in 1979), fifteen families that migrated there in the 1990s, and seven that entered during the twenty-first century. What linked the lives of these families was their eventual settlement in one of several affluent black middle-class suburban enclaves. The most well known of these areas, the city of Bowie, was the strongest magnet. Beyond this commonality, their individual stories varied. For those who entered (or stayed) in Prince George's County during the 1980s, it required two to four moves to reach their final destination. The 1990s migrants completed their journey in an average of just two moves, while most of those entering the county between 2000 and 2004 settled directly in one of these neighborhoods. Combined, their stories help us understand the development of new middle-class suburbs.

Part of the background to this story was the geographic and residential changes occurring in the county during the 1980s and beyond. Prince George's County maintained a rural character longer than other local counties. Against this background of spaciousness in the 1980s, builders began erecting new developments with upscale homes that matched those in the more affluent counties. White residents occupied the first homes built but were followed quickly by middle-class African Americans.

THE EARLY MIGRANTS OF THE 1980S

"In Boston, only whites lived in such houses." While most families I interviewed moved several times within the county, the first move into the county—or the decision to remain in the county—was the most consequential. This move represented a decision to choose *this* place, *this* county above all the other surrounding counties in Maryland and nearby Virginia. They bypassed Montgomery County to the west, a county that, along with Fairfax, Virginia, is one of the most affluent in the nation and home to one

of the best public school systems. Prince George's County also represented a choice over Howard County to the north, which is home to Columbia, a planned city founded by the Rouse Company in 1967, which is popular enough to be the choice of thousands of residents who commute twenty-six miles daily to their jobs in Washington, D.C. Nearby Anne Arundel County and Washington, D.C., also merited passes. For families who came from out of state, Prince George's County represented a major regional shift from places like Boston, Chicago, Charlotte, New Orleans, Iowa, Virginia, and West Virginia. Why did these families select Prince George's County, a county that in many ways was the least attractive choice in the region?

Of the nine early movers, only four came from other states, one couple from Boston, another from Iowa, one from West Virginia, and a fourth from nearby Alexandria, Virginia. The other five families had been in the area for some time, in either D.C. or Prince George's County. All were newlyweds when they decided to either rent or buy a condominium or townhouse for their first residence in Prince George's County. Edith Jamison explained, "I've been here all my life." Her husband, from Guyana, had moved into the county with his family in 1960 at age eleven. When they married in 1979, the Jamisons bought a condominium in Temple Hills, Prince George's County. It was an uncomplicated decision.

Sometimes either the husband or wife had moved into Prince George's County earlier when still single. Richard Andrew moved into Prince George's from D.C. when he was twenty-one. He rented an apartment in Landover, an area of Prince George's County with a small black population. Kay Berry remembered that she had moved with her family from D.C. to Prince George's County when she was only seven or eight years old, adding, "And I just resided in the county with my parents until we got married." The couple continued living with her parents for a year before renting an apartment in a College Park complex not distant from the University of Maryland. There they remained for one year before purchasing a starter home in Largo.

The Harrison and Matthews families presented a different pattern for these early middle-class settlers in Prince George's County. Frank Harrison, from Brooklyn, attended the University of Maryland "because it was so cheap" and remained in the area after graduation. In 1983, he met Joyce, who lived nearby in Mount Rainier, a small suburban city in the county. After marrying in 1987, they bought a townhouse in Largo. Although they did not look at other counties, their residential choice was more complicated than that of the previous two couples.

LANDRY: So I would like to know how you decided to move here [Prince George's County].

FRANK: We liked the setting when we moved out to Largo. It was a brand-new development. There was only one or two models. Right there across from the new Giant. We were just riding around.

JOYCE: We were arguing.

FRANK: We were arguing because I had shown her a place that was in Dodge City.

JOYCE: Up on Landover Road, they had these townhouses, but we had an argument because I wanted to live in D.C. in an older house. Michigan Park. Then I saw this other older house in Cheverly that was perfect; he didn't want it. And since he had more money than I did. At the time—

LANDRY: Money talks.

JOYCE: And you know what walks. So I guess I had to go. But after we looked, though, I was glad.

LANDRY: Did you consult other people?

JOYCE: No.

FRANK: We wanted something brand-new. I wanted something with no maintenance. So we said oh, let's get a brand-new townhome.

LANDRY: So this was being built?

FRANK: It was being built, over in Largo. Because our salaries were so low, we did not qualify for the mortgage at the time. So one of our friends, one of our church friends, said, "I know an individual who can get you financed." So that's how we got the home. US Homes had rejected us.

They bought the townhouse for $87,000 and later sold it for $121,000.

Originally from West Virginia, Cynthia Matthews met her future husband, Henry, while both were attending West Virginia University. After graduation, she came to live and work in D.C., where Henry had grown up. For a while, both rented apartments in different parts of the city, but when they married, Prince George's County was their choice. Cynthia, who knew little about Prince George's County, thought it a good contrast to the busier D.C.

LANDRY: What made you choose to come to Prince George's
    County, to move into Prince George's County?
CYNTHIA: For me I just wanted a suburban area because I'm from
    West Virginia and I was just used to the quiet. I lived in
    Southeast D.C., and it was a little too much for me, and I just
    needed a quieter area. This was closer. I knew about Suitland.
    I drove around. I didn't know very much about Montgomery
    County. I guess because Prince George's was so close to South-
    east. I just liked the apartment area.

Interestingly, none of these couples mentioned the black middle class when discussing their decision to settle in Prince George's County. They made choices that seemed logical and straightforward, given their experiences in the area. Near the end of the decade, however, a critical mass of middle-class blacks coalesced in the county. This was especially true of Mitchellville, the community David Dent wrote about in his 1992 *New York Times Magazine* article.

This budding reputation proved decisive to the Douglas family's decision to move from across the Potomac River in Alexandria, Virginia, in 1987 to a townhouse in Prince George's County. James explained their decision in some detail.

JAMES: For me personally, it was a comfort thing. Being around a lot of whites, riding the bus, commuting back and forth, sometimes I found myself on the bus, sitting alone. Everybody would be standing in the aisle; no one sat beside me. And that was a very uncomfortable feeling for me, and I said, maybe I need more flavor in my life. But that was one of the deciding factors in coming over here.

LANDRY: How about you, Mary?

MARY: Well, with me, I didn't have any problems with Alexandria. But, again, as my husband said, we realized that we could get more over here as opposed to paying rent over there. So, you know we made that move over here. And I have not regretted it.

Once they decided, the choice went smoothly, as the following exchange shows.

LANDRY: Did you consider some other place, Montgomery or Howard or Fairfax?

JAMES: No.

MARY: No.

JAMES: One of my friends had recently gotten into real estate, and he suggested a place that he showed us, and we just didn't question anything else.

While it was the husband who drove their move, in the case of Julia and Roy Bell, it was the wife who initiated the move from Boston.

LANDRY: So, what made you choose Prince George's County?

JULIA: The black middle class. Because they didn't have one there [in Boston]. I found that through my experience that there were blacks who were middle class, but they were fragmented, and there was no sense of community.

LANDRY: In Boston, you mean?

JULIA: In Boston. And I found that here, that sense of community, where black folks were raising their children in an environment around other black children, and they were going to school together. Of course, we came here and we found out that the school system had some serious challenges in Prince George's County. But that [the black middle class], for me, was a selling point to move to the county.

The Bells settled in South Bowie in 1989, which by this time was a growing enclave of upper-middle-class blacks. New communities were sprouting up everywhere with impressive-looking houses and interesting sounding names like Kingsford, King's Forest, Covington Manor, and Grovehurst. Many of these new developments were already primarily black. Their search for a house brought surprises. Recounting part of this process, Julia remarked with astonishment, "We were riding around looking at houses, not knowing about Montgomery, Anne Arundel. We kept saying, where are the white people? We didn't see any."

"They had white people?" Roy asked.

Julia added, "All you really saw in Boston, in these kinds of houses, were [whites]. You had maybe, *maybe* had one black family. But they were majority white living like this. Black people didn't live like this." Within this environment, their final choice of a neighborhood was pragmatic: "Just solely about the house and the area, being close to D.C. You could get into D.C. You could get into Baltimore."

THE MIGRANTS OF THE 1990S

By 1990, the demography of Prince George's County had shifted dramatically. From 37 percent of the county's population in 1980, the African American community had grown to 50 percent, with a significant proportion in the middle class. At the same time, the 50/50 racial mix held out the possibility to observers that Prince George's County would differ from other places, that it would, at last, be a showcase of demographic racial balance, a melting-pot suburb, that it was possible for blacks and whites to live side by side in harmony. This was not to be the case. The winds of change already in motion would soon result in an even more radical remake of the county's landscape and would carry both groups in different directions toward different goals. For middle-class African American families, it would represent an abandonment of the search for residential integration—so fiercely fought for at the end of the civil rights movement—for a *new* type of place with majority or completely black middle-class neighborhoods. For whites, who were never really committed to racial residential or school integration, it would mean flight to other more desirable places. Both trends accelerated during the 1990s and beyond.

There were two types of movers during the 1990s: those who had moved into Prince George's County (or had chosen to stay) for the first time in the 1980s and those who moved into the county during the 1990s. Most of these couples were newlyweds when they selected Prince George's County. They were college-educated professionals beginning their careers, some with salaries that Frank Harrison said "were so low we didn't qualify for the mortgage at the time." They first rented apartments or bought condominiums or townhouses. Except for the one family that moved directly into Bowie in 1989, within one to five years, the lure of home ownership led the renters of the 1980s to become homeowners and motivated those who had purchased condominiums or townhouses to move into single-family homes. The homes they bought were starter homes where they had their first child and often a second. The need for more space motivated a third move, while others moved because of deterioration in the community. At times both the need for more space and a deteriorating community prompted a move. Still others were driven by the desire to experience progress in their lives.

Clarice and Henry Matthews, who had first rented in Suitland in 1979 and then bought a townhouse in Forestville, were an example of a family that moved for a combination of reasons. As their two boys grew, the family was squeezed for space. Henry noted, "When we purchased the townhouse it was a quiet area over in Forestville, new at that time. And then we had two boys. So as they grew the house got smaller, the townhouse; and so we were looking still in the area because it's convenient to downtown D.C. where we both work in the city."

The next move took them into Bowie in 1992. As their story unfolded, it was clear their journey to Bowie had been more complicated than a move for more space, important as that was. Their decision to leave their apartment in Suitland was also because the neighborhood had "started deteriorating." According to Cynthia, "You could see the area [Suitland] starting to go down. That was kind of when we started looking for the townhouse. We went to Forestville, which was a little better. I mean still not quite but it was a good start." Thirteen years after first settling into Suitland, life had changed to the extent that Henry could say, "So it's time we move on. Let's see if we can go to the next level. Let's step up a little bit more when, I don't want to say we moved a little farther out into Prince George's County but I guess that's exactly what we did. We moved on the other side of the beltway into Prince George's County."

"Stepping up" and "the other side of the beltway" are important issues in this complex story of the most affluent black middle-class suburb. The area of Prince George's County *inside the beltway* is contiguous to Southeast D.C., long plagued by poverty and crime. During the 1980s, some of the residential spillover into Prince George's from Southeast D.C. brought a measure of the social problems of the Southeast, including poverty and crime. Earlier, Prince George's County inside the beltway had attracted many new movers. Some areas like Landover had experienced new development, including a new mall and new housing. Eventually, the mall closed in 2002 because of the declining community. These changes led one man to suggest that there were "two Prince George's": one poor and crime ridden inside the beltway, the other affluent in Bowie outside the beltway. The idea of "stepping up" also brings into focus the motivation of class.

By the end of the 1990s, most of the couples who had moved into Prince George's during the 1980s had found their way to black middle-class neighborhoods in Bowie or Upper Marlboro.

For some, the journey was long, stretching through three or four moves over ten or more years. The Jamisons, one of the eight families who moved into the county in the 1980s, only arrived in the Woodmore neighborhood of Bowie in 2004. This family also felt they were "stepping up." "All our purchases have just been to go to the next step," Edith explained of their moves.

As we move further into the 1990s, the black middle-class community continued growing in size and figured more and more into the decisions of those migrating into the county. Still, race and the growing black middle-class community were not the only motivations influencing these moves. Affordability loomed large in the calculus of those opting for Prince George's over the other surrounding counties. Class, convenience, and proximity to families also found their way into discussions.

Race, Class, and Affordability

The Gardners offer a good example of the multiple factors weighed by those who migrated to the county during the 1990s. They married in 1988 in Montgomery County, where they initially rented an apartment. Although their individual motivations differed, they moved into Prince George's County in 1990 to purchase a new townhouse in Mitchellville. For Karen, this was a "very conscious decision" about which she spoke forcefully and enthusiastically.

KAREN: We did make a *conscious decision* to move to Prince George's County. We were pretty much newly married, and so schools and that kind of thing were not a consideration. I wanted to live in a county that was predominantly black and those blacks being pretty affluent as well.

LANDRY: And what about your decision, Morris?

MORRIS: For me it was more about money than anything else. I think that affordability of the things that we could get in Prince George's County versus the things in Montgomery County at that particular time. I still think, probably now, we got a lot more. Particularly as far as the house.

LANDRY: So you went from an apartment to a townhouse. Were you looking for more space?

KAREN: We were, but we were also looking to buy. Because we were renting our apartment and we had been married for what, two years. So we were looking to buy, to purchase a home for all the reasons you buy.

The Gardners wanted to buy a "single-family house" when they first moved into Prince George's County in 1990 but found that "it was a little bit out of our price range." They settled instead on a townhouse in a new development in Mitchellville where the builders had not yet broken ground. It was six years and two births later when they found their dream single-family house, also in Bowie.

KAREN: So this was all new, and we really liked this house. 'Cause we had a lot of things in mind for what we wanted for the house. And we liked the neighborhood as well, so it was just a win-win.

Morris's concern for affordability was again apparent.

MORRIS: And the house was $100,000 cheaper than it was in Montgomery County.

LANDRY: The same model house?

KAREN: The exact same model. But interestingly enough, a lot of the basic features like the hardware that you see in our house is considered an upgrade in Prince George's County.

I was to repeatedly hear that houses in Prince George's County cost $50,000 to $100,000 less than the same houses in Montgomery or Fairfax County. As the above exchange suggests, while that was generally true, in some cases at least, Prince George's homes may have had fewer amenities and required owners to add on or pay for upgrades.

Like the Gardners, the Brodys moved into the county in 1990. Beyond this, their stories differed. Rose Brody was "a native Prince Georgian" who lived there continually except for the years she went away to college. She even spent a semester abroad in Paris as a student. Her husband's history was more complicated. Charles was born in the District, moved to Prince George's with his family when he was nine years old, and lived there until he, too, went away to college. After college, he settled in the District until he married in 1990 and moved back to Prince George's County. Rose and Charles joked about the wedding day.

CHARLES: She wouldn't let me kiss her at the wedding.
ROSE: That's not true! Well, he had "Help me" written on the back of his shoes, so . . .
LANDRY: He had what?
ROSE: "Help me." . . . I'm teasing. No, he didn't. But he told me that if I were late he wouldn't marry me. So it's the one time in my life I've been on time.

As they recounted their decision to buy a townhouse in Landover, neither race nor class came up, although they mentioned cost.

LANDRY: Well, what was the reason when you finally made your decision? Was it due to family, or what was it?
ROSE: For me it was "get it done." I could have used more guidance.
LANDRY: Did you look around? I mean, did you actually look at other places?
CHARLES: No. From my standpoint it was the best option at the time.
LANDRY: Meaning what?
CHARLES: Meaning, at that time in the housing market, it was not very easy to find something. I think interest rates at that point were around 10 percent. It was a tough market, and it was hard

for us to find a place that both of us could get happy with, and I think that was the only place both of us could get happy with.

ROSE: It was a really big townhouse. And we could afford it.

CHARLES: Right, right. There were some advantages to living there in terms of its marketability going forward, so it seemed to be the best decision.

The Brodys lived in their Landover townhouse for nine years before moving to the Covington Manor development in Bowie. In our discussion of their motives for this second move, class came up, but only obliquely, as the following dialogue shows.

LANDRY: What led you to move?

ROSE: Just the change in the neighborhood.

CHARLES: Yes, the change in the neighborhood. And I think you wanted more space.

ROSE: Wanted to step up, and the people in the community didn't share our values about upkeep. The value of quiet and personal space. . . . Quite frankly, as we matured, we saw that different areas were treated in different ways. And that most things—it doesn't matter what your individual home or abode is like—are driven by zip code. For example, as soon as we moved here and gave our Bowie address, I think our car insurance was cut in half. I don't know if our health insurance rates were affected. I have no idea about that.

CHARLES: Life insurance.

ROSE: Life insurance was affected. Just the type of mail that we would receive. The type of solicitations. We were changing and growing and maturing, but the area around us was not. And we found that there were no amenities. There was no place to, for example, go to the movies. There was just nothing. Not even upscale but midscale. There was just like a broad assumption that everybody was economically depressed.

Like Cynthia and Henry Matthews, Rose and Charles Brody had made the move to the "other side of the beltway."

So, it was the search for a middle-class area in Bowie that led to their second move. It was also the school that their daughter attended that kept them in Prince George's County. It is clear, also, that this was a different, more perceptive, more mature couple that was making decisions at this time. There were, then, a large number of factors weighed in residential decisions, including dissatisfaction with a current neighborhood, the need for more living space, a desire for a neighborhood with certain characteristics such as racial and class composition, and affordability.

People like Us

Although people often mentioned the price advantage of buying a house in Prince George's County compared to Montgomery or Fairfax, most of the couples who settled in the county during the 1990s and beyond cited race as part of their motivation, some more forcefully than others. Both Alfred and Charlene Johnson settled in Prince George's County while single and attending the University of Maryland. She bought a condominium and he a house while still single. Both had lived in a variety of places, including Montgomery County. When asked why they stayed in Prince George's County after their marriage, Alfred answered.

ALFRED: I would say that one of the major factors of staying in Prince George's County is pretty much because of the black concentration, professional black concentration.
CHARLENE: People like us, a lot of people like us. And you could buy your pantyhose your color, without having to look too hard. And your hair-care products.
ALFRED: Just the small little things make, you know, a big, big difference.

Like the Johnsons, Laura and Robert Williams shared a similar attraction to Prince George's County, although Laura had lived in Montgomery County all her life. After a year in an apartment in Greenbelt as newlyweds, in 1993 they moved to Mitchellville.

ROBERT: Once we got there [Greenbelt], we realized that wasn't where we wanted to stay for a while. But we knew that Mitchellville was a great place to be. It was up-and-coming. I mean it's been around, established, there had been a lot of building.

LAURA: We had friends who had actually just bought a new town-home there, so we started looking. We actually built a town-home, and we moved there in August of '94. We were definitely planning a family, and Mitchellville was a nice area for young families, young African American families. So we definitely wanted to live in a neighborhood where we could be raising our kids together. Like minds, you know. Like goals and aspirations. So Mitchellville was very impressive, particularly for me because I grew up in this area. I knew about Montgomery County versus Prince George's County. It was always a thing. I really never came to Prince George's County when I was growing up.

LANDRY: So what's particularly attractive for young families to move into Mitchellville or Prince George's County?

ROBERT: Because there were other people like us—African Americans that were starting to do the same things that we were doing.

LAURA: Driven, progressive. Like minds. They're educated. There was a lot of development going on that I know I didn't see in Montgomery County. It was focused; it seemed focused on African Americans.

For some, their past experiences figured into the mix of motivations. This was true for Jerry Brooks, who moved with his wife to Prince George's County in 1996.

LANDRY: You had a preference for Prince George's County when you moved here?

JERRY: I wanted to move to a black county. Prince George's County was the only black county.

LANDRY: Why?

JERRY: I wanted to spend my money in a predominately black county, Prince George's County. I thought they were really progressive. Most of my military career I was in a lot of white counties and white parts of town, and being from Baltimore originally I went to Tuskegee, predominately black, and I wanted to be in a black county. And I thought my kids would also benefit from that too.

Jerry's wife, Denise, expressed more complex motivations, but it was also clear that for her the racial composition of the community mattered.

LANDRY: Did you have a preference after seeing different parts of the area?

DENISE: I did not. It kind of looked all the same to me. And I really didn't research to find out anything about the differences. At that point, we didn't have children and didn't think we were going to have children, and so it wasn't that we were looking for a better school system. It was primarily economically where we could afford to live, and where do we, quote unquote, fit in.

LANDRY: And this felt?

DENISE: And this felt right.

Not all settlers in Prince George's County during the 1980s and '90s were motivated by its growing black middle-class population, however. Christine and Steve Edwards lived for a time in Montgomery County while single and then bought a townhouse in Prince George's County in the late 1980s. When asked about his rationale for buying in Prince George's, Steve replied, "Affordability."

STEVE: I could get more house in Prince George's than I could in Montgomery.

LANDRY: Was there any other consideration for moving into this house?

STEVE: No. That was a big thing. Like I said, I looked at a lot of places in Montgomery. I just didn't find anything that I liked, and then when I walked into the townhouse that I have, I just loved it and just stayed. So it had nothing to do with the county or anything like that in particular. It was just, really it was the fireplace that I bought.

Although it was "affordability" that brought him into the county, not the county itself, why did he stay upon marriage? Again, it was a practical consideration. When he married in 1995, his new bride, Christine, moved in with him. Later, when they bought a house together in 1999, it was a house close by. Christine explained their decision: "Because it was five minutes from our old neighborhood and because our kid's school is down the street, so just trying to stay close to her school."

The location, which provided an easier commute to Christine's work at the Labor Department in the District, also influenced their decision. When I interviewed them in 2007, they were still enthusiastic over the merits of the location, not only convenient to work but to a variety of places.

STEVE: It's close to everything. Where we live, I mean, we can go to New York, we can go to Baltimore, we can just go to Annapolis. So we do a lot of things; we take the girls to a lot of different places in the state. It's real easy to get around, so that's probably the thing I'm most satisfied with.

Role Models

Those couples, like Thomas and Shirley Edison, whose move into Prince George's County was motivated by its concentration of middle-class blacks, often mentioned the benefit of role models for their children.

THOMAS: One of the major reasons for Prince George's County is that it's unique. It's an African American county, and our children can see what they want to become. Like, my brother was here from California, my younger brother was here, stayed with us for about a year. And he's from San Jose, and the experience there is completely opposite, meaning you're one, two, ten, or so in your high school. So you don't get the African American experience. When you go to a dentist, you can't aspire to be a dentist because you don't see me in that profession.

This couple from nearby Montgomery County had settled in Riverdale, a part of Prince George's County that in 1991 was mostly white. Later the neighborhood experienced successive waves of demographic change, and they moved. When I asked why they did not move back to Montgomery County, Shirley answered, "Montgomery County is expensive. And I like Prince George's County. I like being around black people. I moved from North Carolina for that very reason. 'Cause North Carolina, in my little hometown, you had to go to your white doctors, you had your white dentist, white lawyer. Anything professional, it was all white. So you never knew anybody black could do anything, and I was determined my kids wouldn't see that. So now, in Prince George's County, everybody we would go to was black. And they need to see that. They know what they see on TV isn't true life. They'll know the difference."

Peggy Turner, who also moved to the area from North Carolina for work and settled in Prince George's County, spoke enthusiastically about the role models her children had in their community.

PEGGY: I think it is definitely a positive thing for him [her son] to see his neighbors as role models in the professional career sense. If he goes two blocks down [the street] and his neighbor is the director of finance at one of the largest corporations in the area, he can see that there are black CIOs and CEOs and we're not just how people portrayed us on TV. Which is what I grew up with a lot of the time because I didn't have any other distinction from the stereotypes that people presented on TV. Where I grew up, most of the black people were poor. Most of the black people didn't live in houses like this. This was the exception; this was not the norm.

TONY: Yeah, this was the exception.

PEGGY: And here, this is the norm. So I'm hoping he'll have a different paradigm about what he feels are opportunities for him. Not that my mother didn't tell me everything was my opportunity, it's just that living it, and seeing it, and breathing it—I'm hoping his expectations will be, "I can be just like any of them."

Black middle-class migration into Prince George's County was not always without problems. When the Harrisons attempted a second move from Largo to a community in Bowie in 1991, they were met with resistance.

JOYCE: They didn't want us out here really.

FRANK: When we came out here back in 1991, the female white sales agent wouldn't even talk to us.

LANDRY: For this area?

FRANK: Yeah, for this development, back in 1991. So we waited a year later, and we came out and they had a different sales rep. Very nice gentleman, Jewish gentleman.

LANDRY: So what was it that sold you on this neighborhood?

FRANK: Trees, we love trees.

JOYCE: We like trees, and we like nature, and we like the builders' commitment to only cut down enough trees to put the homes up. I don't like to see areas where they knock all the trees down. And then they put homes and they're out in the blazing sun.

FRANK: Plus the price of the homes was cheap. This home, we bought it for $211,000. It took about a year to build.

Although by 1990 Prince George's County had reached a 50/50 demographic balance, many neighborhoods were still mainly or totally white and not welcoming to African Americans of any class. The irony in this case was not lost on the Harrisons.

FRANK: But it was all white. When we came out here looking at the basement and seeing how things were being constructed, some of our [white] neighbors would come over and ask what we did. Where do you work? Very personal questions.

JOYCE: As if we had to answer these questions to qualify.

LANDRY: So most of the neighbors were white.

FRANK: They were all white.

JOYCE: The thing about it that was so strange: the people that were asking. They required all of this stuff for us to get in here and all of this income. And it's like these people were asking us all about our education and what we did. One guy drove for UPS. One guy was a journalist; he had a high school education. It seemed like to people who lived out here we did all this work and all of this saving to get out here in this neighborhood, and here the white people that live in this neighborhood are like firemen. Mostly blue-collar workers.

In the late twentieth and early twenty-first centuries, middle-class blacks finally were able to move into the suburbs in significant numbers. They were now achieving what whites had long claimed as their sole right. It remained unclear, however, what kind of communities would result. Would these suburbs become melting pots, integrated neighborhoods, or predominantly black communities? I explore this question in the following chapter.

3

Changing Neighborhoods

A number of factors help explain the development of black middle-class suburbs in Prince George's County. First, compared with the other surrounding suburban counties of the Washington, D.C., metro area, the more rural and sparsely developed Prince George's County offered builders greater opportunities to erect new developments beginning in the 1980s. Second, already in 1970 Prince George's County had a history of African American residents that was unmatched by other counties. Third, the new developments featured upscale homes that matched those in the surrounding, more densely populated, more affluent counties but were offered at more attractive prices. Although whites were the first to occupy these new neighborhoods, a growing black middle class also saw these new developments as opportunities. As we saw in the previous chapter, some families moved into established developments, while others bought homes as new neighborhoods were forming. Racially, some of these neighborhoods were all white, while others were racially mixed. By 1990, the percentage of blacks in the county had increased to 50 percent. Had Prince George's County become a melting pot?

Myron Orfield and Thomas Luce suggest that the most desirable residential pattern is diverse or integrated because of the greater educational and economic opportunities offered. They also observed that integrated communities are difficult to maintain over a long period. The question in 1990 was whether Prince George's County would remain diverse and integrated, or whether it would become a predominantly black suburban county. When I interviewed the thirty-one couples in 2007, the hope for a stable, racially diverse suburban county was already lost. With over 63 percent black residents, the suburban county had slipped into Orfield and Luce's "predominantly black" category, confirming the difficulty of maintaining a diverse suburb.

White Flight

To understand how racial diversity had declined, I asked couples about the racial composition of their neighborhoods. Their responses made it clear that the growing predominance of middle-class blacks in many neighborhoods was not simply the result of black in-migration. White families were moving out from old and new communities, often as black families moved in. Claudia Gilbert recalled her experience in 1988 by noting, "As we were moving in, they [whites] were moving out." Sometimes respondents could count the number of white families remaining. I asked James and Mary Douglas about the racial composition of the neighborhood into which they moved.

JAMES: Well, this is a new side, and it's always been black. On the other side of the development, whites were in first, and as they built the houses, blacks came in. But now that is slowly changing; they're moving out again.

LANDRY: Who's moving out again?

JAMES: I'd say, whites are, whites are. They're not that many left over here.

MARY: Now, except for the first house when you come in.

JAMES: And he has a "for sale" sign in his yard.

MARY: Matter of fact, that was one of the first houses, I think, in Grove Hurst.

JAMES: Yeah, they've slowly moved out.

A conversation with David and Marlene George about the racial composition of their neighborhood went as follows.

DAVID: As you go through older Bowie, you'll notice tons of "for sale" signs, so it's almost like the blackness is kind of growing virally, you know what I mean?

LANDRY: What about this community? What's the racial composition here?

DAVID: Where we live, all of this, we have one white family.

MARLENE [INCREDULOUSLY]: Where?

DAVID: Right on the corner. They just haven't sold their house yet.

MARLENE: I thought they had moved, but they haven't.

DAVID: No, he's still there.

MARLENE: And there's another white family down the street from them.

DAVID: They're gone.

MARLENE: You're sure?

DAVID: Yeah. They're getting out of Dodge.

MARLENE: We actually don't have any other, no Hispanic neighbors, no Asian neighbors.

DAVID: It's all black, this entire community.

The Howards described the racial transition that had been occurring in their neighborhood.

LANDRY: Is this community 100 percent black, is it mixed, or what is it?

FRANCES: It's about 90 percent.

JOSEPH: Ninety? Seventy-five percent?

FRANCES: Africans, some Caucasians. I can't say how many.

JOSEPH: In Collington Station, it's probably about 75 percent, 80 percent black.

FRANCES: When we moved in [1993], there were more whites.

JOSEPH: When we moved in, it was probably 60 percent white, but just on my street.

FRANCES: There were several.

JOSEPH: On my street we were one, three black families; everybody else white.

FRANCES: Maybe half-and-half. But there are still two or three white couples that are across the street.

JOSEPH: Two white families and Mary. She moved, and then we had 50 percent white to about 50 percent black; and at one point to about 75 percent to 80 percent black in the total community.

By the mid-1990s, many of the recently built communities were largely black, in spite of the 50/50 split in the county at large. The Andrews estimated that the racial composition of the Grove Hurst community in Bowie was a 70/30 black/white mix in 1995. By 2007, it had become "all black," according to the Georges, who had moved into the community in 1997. Some couples spoke of other groups in their communities—most frequently, Asian or Hispanic families. In one neighborhood of Fort Washington with eighty-five homes, the racial/ethnic composition was 85 percent black, 5 percent Asian, and 5 percent white. In another community in Bowie that was 90 percent black, I was told by the Edwins that the other 10 percent included whites, Hispanics, and Asians. Some neighborhoods experienced fluidity along the way. This was the case with a neighborhood in Upper Marlboro where Kay and John Berry had lived for nine years beginning in 1993.

LANDRY: The neighborhood you moved into, you said it was being built and yours was the last house. And that was a largely black neighborhood in Upper Marlboro?

KAY: It was more black than white.

JOHN: It might have been like 60/40 black/white.

KAY: We lived on a cul-de-sac. There was an interracial couple next to us; the woman next to us was black.

JOHN: There was another white couple, Renee and Jim, and before them, the white couple there got divorced.

KAY: Right, and then another white couple moved in, and then directly across, there was always the girls.

KAY: Yeah, Lois and Jane, they were black, and next to them was black, and next to them was white.

JOHN: Well, no, they had the Asian couple.

KAY: Oh, right, Asian. She was Asian, he was Hispanic. So we had all this. This was a cul-de-sac, seven houses.

JOHN: I would say it was like maybe 60/40 if not 50/50.

KAY: But then every time a white couple moved out, a black couple moved in.

LANDRY: Was there a lot of movement then?

KAY: Yes, and there were a couple of foreclosures.

Some of this fluidity subsided over time. The Brodys described their experience after moving into Covington Manor in Bowie in 1999, noting that it had changed little over the years.

LANDRY: When you moved here, what was the racial composition in this neighborhood?

CHARLES: In this particular neighborhood? Probably about 80 percent African American, 20 percent other. A combination of other.

LANDRY: Is it more mixed now?

CHARLES: About the same.

ROSE: 'Cause nobody has really moved. And the people on the first court, they're very close, and what they do is close off the whole cul-de-sac, and all the children converge and play.

Likewise, the Edisons, who moved from Riverdale to Upper Marlboro in 2004, provided a picture of stability in their community.

LANDRY: What was the racial composition like here when you moved in? In 2004?

THOMAS: We made it 50/50.

SHIRLEY: Our neighbors moved in.

THOMAS: Yeah, they changed the neighborhood.

SHIRLEY: That's about the only one, though. There's not a lot of moving in and out of here.

THOMAS: There's no movement.

It was clear that racial statistics at the county level were different from those at the neighborhood level. It is a point that analysts often miss when talking about racial residential patterns. One neighborhood may be integrated, while another has shifted to a predominantly or totally single-race neighborhood. In Prince George's County, the shift since 1990 seemed to track toward predominantly or all black middle-class neighborhoods. It was the outcome of black families moving in and white families moving out as my respondents described. White flight became a subtext to the principal story of the growing concentration of middle-class blacks in Prince George's County over the past three decades. Both stories are important parts of the recent history of the county as well as of other areas of black suburbanization. They are like two sides of the same coin. One cannot understand black middle-class suburbanization in the twenty-first century without understanding both developments.

The white flight that took place in Prince George's County during the 1980s, 1990s, and beyond is part of the broader story of residential patterns and segregation in the United States as told by sociologists Douglas S. Massey and Nancy A. Denton in *American Apartheid*.[1] Piecing together the various threads of in-and-out migration during the 1980s and '90s revealed a growing concentration of upper-middle-class African American families in new and old developments outside the beltway. Although white flight was a major response to the growing black presence in Bowie and other areas, the increasing numbers of African Americans was not the only factor involved.

Busing for School Desegregation and Its Effect on White Flight

Given the history of the United States, the racial composition of public places takes on great importance. After the passage of the

Civil Rights Act in 1964 banning discrimination, many places—restaurants, theaters, beaches, neighborhoods—became contested arenas. As African Americans struggled to exercise their "birthright" to live in any community they chose, whites pushed back with resistance or flight. In Prince George's County, this has been true of both neighborhoods and schools. Many whites left the county in the 1980s and '90s because of their aversion to living side by side with black families. For others, the court-ordered busing to desegregate schools motivated their move. It is against this background that the Harrisons' statements can be understood.

FRANK: The whites actually started moving out about four or five years ago. Their kids started getting older; they didn't want their kids to go to our schools.

JOYCE: And the man across the street said that when his child got big, he didn't want his kid in Prince George's public schools because he didn't want him to be a minority. He wanted him to be comfortable.

Ironically, Rita and Herman Madison, who moved their family from Fairfax, Virginia, to Bowie, expressed a similar sentiment regarding their daughter.

RITA: We were looking to buy a house. And we thought we could get more house for our money. We liked there was diversity in Prince George's County. I think where we lived in northern Virginia it was primarily white, and we didn't want our daughter, who we had at the time, to go to a school that was predominately white.

HERMAN: To be the only black kid in class.

RITA: Right. 'Cause my sister and I . . . I remember when we lived in northern Virginia, being the only black kids in a school at one particular time in Alexandria. And we had to meet with the principal and the teacher, and it was a big deal to integrate us into the school. But it wasn't a scarring situation. I mean, we remember the school. We had neighbors that were great friends.

But we just didn't want that pressure on them [their children]. And so that was another decision that led us to the county: income, trying to get more house for our money, trying to be in a more diverse area. We weren't necessarily looking for an all-black neighborhood; we just wanted to be in a comfortable mix. So those were some of the reasons.

There is a stark contrast in the experience of the mother integrating a white public school in the past, and the experience the couple wanted for their daughter. There is likewise some irony in the desires of both black and white families to "protect" their children. Protect them from what? On the one hand, there was a black family who did not want their daughter to experience the isolation and pressure of being a minority in what might be a hostile white school environment; on the other hand, a white family fearing the discomfort that its child might face as a minority in a primarily black classroom. Their personal dilemmas reflected the larger struggle unfolding around them, the struggle for a comfortable place to live viewed against the background of our racial history.

The British sociologist Frank Parkin argued that modern class struggles play out through proxy battles for control of institutions.[2] In Prince George's County during the late twentieth century, both race and class struggles were fought over control of the schools. Both white and black families saw this struggle in terms of their children's futures. Several couples I interviewed commented on the broader dimensions of this conflict, which in time became a struggle for control of the political institution as well. The Hamiltons did not know the racial composition of their neighborhood when they moved into Saddle Brook in 2001, but they perceived that it was a critical time, a "turning point."

LANDRY: Do you know what the racial composition was, roughly, when you guys moved in?
BRAD: Like in this city or . . . ?

LANDRY: In the neighborhood?

DEBBIE: I don't know.

BRAD: I don't know the particular neighborhood. I know what Bowie was when we moved here. I mean Bowie in general was at that time 40 percent black. Something like that, twenty to forty. In fact, it was kind of a turning point when we moved here. It was a turning point when a lot of racial tension over the city government was turning over because the composition of the county was changing. So the composition of the city board, the mayor, those kinds of things were changing. It was all over the papers.

The Georges related a story of the attempted secession of largely white north Bowie, often referred to as "old Bowie" in contrast to the new, growing black developments in south Bowie. David noted, "One of the issues that happened that I thought was pretty amusing: Older Bowie is mostly Caucasian folks, and they were upset because they thought the new Bowie, which is predominately black folks getting these huge houses, was getting all the attention. And they felt their services declined, so they went to the city council to get themselves annexed to Ann Arundel County. Didn't work. They said, 'You want to get annexed to Ann Arundel County? Go move to Ann Arundel County 'cause it's staying the same.'"

The Rise and Fall of Busing

Until the 1954 Supreme Court's decision in *Brown v. Board of Education*, Prince George's County's school system operated under an 1872 Maryland law that separated black and white children: separate schools, buses, teachers, and supervisors. This Maryland law, in principle, was nullified with the Supreme Court's decision. It did not end so simply. While the county school board initially expressed its commitment to follow the dictates of the Supreme Court's decision, it did not follow the suggestions of its own study group, the Fact-Finding Committee to Study the Problems of

Desegregation in Prince George's County. Like school districts in many other southern and border states, it adopted a "freedom of choice" plan that placed the burden of desegregation on black parents, who had to request to transfer their children to a majority white school. Poor publicity of the process, together with frequent refusals of parents' requests, ensured the failure of the "freedom of choice" approach.

Two events brought matters to a head: the involvement of the Department of Health, Education, and Welfare, and lawsuits from a variety of groups. The most important of these lawsuits came from a group of black parents in 1971. It led to a 1973 federal court decision declaring the school board's desegregation plan to be noncompliant with the 1964 Civil Rights Act and ordering it to draw up a new desegregation plan with busing. With this court order, Prince George's County joined other jurisdictions in the southern and border states in using busing for school desegregation. The size of the county's school system, the tenth largest in the country, drew national attention. None of the other suburban counties in the D.C. metropolitan area adopted busing. Although the county was spared the conflict and violence of Little Rock, Arkansas, busing was popular with neither black nor white parents. Concern over the negative effects on black children dogged the process, and the program hastened the flight of white families to racially segregated areas of the county and to nearby counties.

After twenty-six years of court-ordered busing for school desegregation, the practice ended in 2002. Ironically, it was a suit filed by black middle-class families that hammered the final nail in the coffin of forced busing. In its latest phase, the school board had introduced special academic programs to attract white students to largely black schools. Often some of these slots, reserved for whites, went unfilled but were not opened to black students, angering their parents. The end of court-ordered busing for school integration reflected a new reality in the county, a turning away from a black commitment to school integration toward a demand for excellence for their children regardless of the racial mix of the school.

The Demise of Integration?

If many middle-class black families gave up on school integration, how did they feel about residential integration? It was clear that a high percentage of Prince George's white residents had no interest. For middle-class blacks, residential integration had been a goal over the preceding decades. At times, it was difficult to untangle individual motives. Was it the struggle for the right to live wherever one wished, the goal of living in places with better resources, or a desire to live peacefully among whites in integrated neighborhoods? Whatever the individual reasons that motivated those who fought these battles, was it still important to the black middle-class families who moved into the Prince George's County suburbs?

By the mid-1990s, important political changes were occurring in Prince George's County that promised to confer more political control to black residents. The last white county executive, Parris Glendening, served the county from 1982 to 1994. In 1994, Wayne Curry became the first black county executive of Prince George's County and the only African American county executive in the United States. He was followed by other black county executives. It is against this changing background that I discussed attitudes about residential integration with the thirty-one couples I interviewed.

Although the couples rarely brought up the question of integration, when I broached the subject it was clear they had well-formed opinions that reflected their lives in affluent predominantly black middle-class neighborhoods. The ensuing conversations were some of our longest. Their positions coalesced around three points of view. There were some who thought that residential integration was "a plus" or that it did not matter. Within this group were those who clarified that, if residential integration occurred, it would have to be whites moving into *their* neighborhoods. The second group had no interest in residential integration, stressing the comfort of living in a black community. The third and largest group included those couples who turned the conversation to the benefits of diversity for their children, who would have to manage life in a largely white world, even though they did not need integration for themselves.

In the first group, answers were not always consistent or were conditional. Sandra James at first said she liked integration because "I don't like separation. Because I don't like people thinking they're better than the other person when we're all supposed to be equal." When asked if it mattered whether her neighborhood was integrated or not, she replied, "It doesn't matter to me." Her husband, Keith, who agreed with this sentiment, emphasized that their criteria in choosing a neighborhood were safety and an "environment" they wanted, adding, "And if that neighborhood was diverse, then that's a plus." At the time of the interview, their neighborhood was divided about 50/50 between blacks and whites.

Jennifer and Troy Roberts likewise were open to residential integration. Their neighborhood of 171 homes, with 65 percent black and 35 percent white families when they first settled there in 1997, was now 85 percent black and only 15 percent white. Troy's immediate response to my question on integration was "Me, honestly, I'm okay with it, 'cause the world is diverse." He then qualified his statement by stressing that he was thinking of his middle-class neighborhood but he "might be opposed" if the white neighbors were not middle class. Jennifer responded in a similar fashion as her husband, observing that she had grown up in an integrated community. When I suggested that she could move to nearby Howard or Montgomery County, with higher concentrations of whites, she replied, "Yeah, I could. But I don't find that it's that important to have to relocate to be around an integrated community. It's not that important to me. It's nice to have if it's there, but if it's not it doesn't bother me one way or the other."

Some couples stressed the advantage of living in an integrated community. This was the case with the Edisons, whose neighborhood was split 50/50 between blacks and whites. For Shirley, it was "good having diversity in the neighborhood 'cause it's like the picture's a little warmer. When you leave here, you need to know how to interact with all kinds of people." She continued, stressing the benefits of having other groups in the neighborhood: "But if you don't know how to interact, if you don't know how to interact with a certain people, you're gonna feel left out, you're gonna feel rejected. But you can stand your ground amongst any people [if you know how to interact]."

My conversation with the Berrys made it clear they were discussing residential integration with the awareness they lived in an affluent black upper-middle-class area. With that in mind, Kay wished there were "a little bit more of it [integration], because the world is not all black, and my kids have to be able to" manage in this world. Nevertheless, her desire for more whites in her community coexisted with the knowledge that at "this historical moment blacks are more equal" so their arrival "wouldn't be a gentrification thing." Unlike blacks who sought integration in earlier decades, they spoke from an advantageous position. While acknowledging that whites had more wealth than blacks, Kay added, "Nobody's just going to come into our neighborhood and just take over. That being the case, we do want a little bit more diversity . . . as long as we maintain the power balance."

John felt differently about residential integration. His remarks, after his wife's on the "power balance," could not have been more different: "I don't know, Dr. Landry. I don't know if I need more white folks in our neighborhood. I'll be honest. To the extent I talk to them at work, when I come home, I don't need more of them here."

At one point, my conversation with the Berrys on neighborhood residential integration turned to the city of Bowie. Remembering his experience growing up in a diverse but spatially separated Pittsburgh, John emphasized that Bowie was similarly divided into "pockets" of blacks and whites rather than integrated neighborhoods. Bowie, he said, was "the tale of two cities" with separated black and white areas, and he recalled that he came across an elementary school in Bowie where all the kids were white. Then the conversation turned to Allen Pond Park, a place where blacks and whites encounter each other for celebrations like Bowie Fest and Bowie Day. Kay continued with a fuller description:

"Thursdays they have movie night in the summer or Sunday concerts, and you go there and you think, 'Okay, this is the American Dream' 'cause you look around and it's everybody. And the interactions are—we aren't all falling all over each other or whatever, but they're warm enough. If you see somebody, you're saying 'Hi,' so it's halting but it's more than a lot of people have. My white friends live in white places. My black friends are a lot of times in all-black places. So I do appreciate what we have."

If some couples were open to residential integration, even though only conditionally, there were those in the second group who had no use for it. Although his wife suggested that integration increased property value, Roy Bell criticized the idea "that being with white people is going to make us better. I think that's a fallacy." He thought that integration has been harmful to black communities and, after noting that whites often move out when blacks move in, wondered, "Why do we keep doing this? It makes no sense." Claudia Gilbert expressed the same sentiment. "When your work environment tends not to be that way [i.e., integrated], you want to be able to come home and relax with your people." As with Claudia, the work experience of the Johnsons also appeared to influence their views on residential integration. Both described challenging and uncomfortable work experiences with whites. Alfred, who had worked in sales for a Fortune 500 company as one of only three blacks in a group of eighty, complained of always having to mind his "p's and q's." His wife contrasted living among whites in the North, while her father was in the military, with her adult work experience. As an account manager, she found working with whites stressful. "I had Howard University Hospital for ten years of my life, and it was my biggest hospital account. And it was so different than when I have to work with white people. And it's not even the doctors, it's the [white] people at my company. They don't want you to be smarter than them. They don't want you to outshine them." Their answers to my question about residential integration were not surprising. "I don't necessarily need to live around white people," Charlene Johnson emphasized. "No. I mean integration is okay, if it happens, if white people moved around me." Her husband confirmed this sentiment: "Right, that's the way I want it. I want them to move into my neighborhood, and we stay the majority, and they're the ones that are trying to assimilate into the community." Charlene agreed: "They have more of a problem living amongst us, a whole bunch of us, than the other way around. You don't see us moving out because there were five white families there."

Tony Turner, who had moved from Charlotte, North Carolina, in 2001 and settled in a black community in Perrywood, confessed that residential integration was "not even on my mind." What he had wanted, he emphasized, was "to have a neighborhood that, as a professional, I could move in without problems, with no drama, without having to go to the aid station and get lawyers." When I asked Dorothy Smith her views on residential integration, she replied, "I don't care." Then after a pause she said, "I wouldn't mind if it were more integrated but not necessarily white. More people of color, different colors. You know, Indian, Asian. I think a more diverse community just can only be better." Then she asked, "Did that thing [residential integration] die?" Her husband, Arthur, replied, "I don't know." To which she remarked with mock surprise and laughter: "I'm sorry [that it did]."

Darrell Snow was likewise uninterested in residential integration. Having grown up in a black middle-class neighborhood in Chicago, he was happy to replicate that experience in Bowie in 2004. Although he and his wife had met white couples through their daughter's integrated school, gymnastic class, and summer camp, they confessed there had been no exchange of home visits with white families. It was not something he was "looking for per se." Nor did it seem imminent, as he added, "My friends are my friends, and, hey, if I find a white guy that likes hip-hop music, that is interested in social issues, political issues, and we have the same viewpoints, I don't mind sitting down and talking to that person, but to this point I don't have that. I haven't found that buddy yet. So you know." His wife, Susan, was likewise uninterested. When I asked her how she felt about residential integration, her response was indirect. "I like services. I'll tell you that you get that just in general being in a suburban area as opposed to an urban area, black or white, I think. I like the fact that we can go to the store, and everything's accessible. That wasn't the case in Chicago. And that's what I used to call and complain about. And/ or if I wanted to go to a health food store, this or that. So I was happy to see that I could (a) come back and be around *black people*, and (b) still have the services."

In the third group were the couples who were not at all interested in residential integration for themselves but who often felt differently about their children. Charlene Johnson declared, "I don't necessarily need to live around white people, no." At another point in our conversation she confessed, "I always feel like Jackie [her daughter] needs her integration dose. So in the summer, I send her to integrated camps at least once or twice. I just feel like she will have to learn how to live amongst them." I often heard similar statements. Couples who considered residential integration only conditionally or who opposed it often felt it had value for their children. This seeming contradiction resulted from their concern about their children's future. Their own experience told them it was necessary to know how to manage in white environments like work and that one day their children would meet this challenge. Preparing them for this included integrated summer camps, integrated schools, and sometimes integrated neighborhoods.

Judy Harrington recounted the dissimilar experiences of her two daughters in the work world, which she felt resulted from their different education:

> The neighborhood, I don't think it matters. The school, I think it matters somewhat. I think because my older daughter, when she went to school in Prince George's County, we transferred her to private school but it was still a predominately black private school. She went to a private black college, and she got a job with Liz Claiborne. She wasn't used to dealing with them. She didn't know how white girls could be in a competitive environment. So she had to learn to put her guards up, and she just said: "Ma, I didn't have a clue how to deal with this." So

I think that is important. My other daughter, she goes to Georgetown Visitation [Preparatory School], so she deals with it constantly. The problem I have is what it does to them. It tears down their confidence level. You know, because their confidence—white girls are so competitive, whites period are so competitive—most of the time you really have to know how to deal with it. She learned how to deal with it early. My other daughter, she didn't, and it just made her whole experience, her internship, terrible because she didn't know how to deal with it. And so I think it is important in schools to have that diversity so they can learn and just not grow up in a totally black environment and put them out into the world, and they're not used to dealing with the competitiveness.

Charlene and Judy reflect one of the major dilemmas that black middle-class families face in Prince George's County. Having created African American communities to which they can retreat after work, they still face important challenges. Preparing their children for a future in a mostly white society is one of the greatest. Some parents spoke of preparation to deal with the "mixture" their children will find in the "real" world or workplace; others praised the benefits of exposure to other cultures. Keith James, who supported school integration and even busing to achieve more diverse school populations, represented the former group.

KEITH: Do I support the nature of integration and busing? Absolutely. Because I think in the realities of life we're gonna face that. I think, you know, when youngsters go to college, depending upon which college they go to, you're gonna probably find a mixture. When they're going to the job market, you're gonna in most cases find a mixture.

SANDRA: They're definitely gonna find a mixture.

KEITH: So I think the more that we can prepare them to deal with the dynamics and the diversity and that demographics, I think the better off that we are. So for those reasons alone I think I would support, you know, busing individuals and balancing it out.

Several parents with children in a racially and ethnically diverse Montessori school emphasized the benefits of cultural exposure for their children. In the following exchange, the Georges spoke of their child's exposure to cultural rather than just racial diversity.

MARLENE: The school Tyler's going to is a Montessori school.
DAVID: The main reason why he goes—
MARLENE: Is the learning method that was recommended. But also, it's a very diverse school. Dr. Landry, I have no idea where the Indian people live around here, but there's a lot of Indian people, not Native American people, but I guess Eastern Indian people. And Asian kids go there, Hispanic kids go there. And again, I don't ever see any of these people in the store, in the Giant or the Safeway up the street; I never see any of them. But at that school, it's so many different cultures. I do not know— because I don't know a lot about little people and how they develop—how much this is gonna affect Tyler's perception of the world, but hopefully it'll let him know there's more than just people that look like Mommy and Daddy and the rest of our family members.

The Tuckers, who had children in a Montessori school, also praised the value of black children's exposure to cultural diversity.

LINDA: I think the school that our children go to is very diverse. Very diverse, very. They are at Robert Goddard, where half of the school is a Montessori school; the other half is a French immersion school.
LANDRY: This is a public school?
LINDA: This is a public school, a magnet program in Prince George's County. So I like the fact that they are getting more diversity because I think there are a lot of Indians that go to the school, a lot of Hispanics, a lot of whites, a lot of Africans, a lot of blacks. I mean it's really, really mixed. You know, with our children . . . She says her two best friends—one is Indian, one is white. I like the fact that they learn about the different cultures of each. She

can come and tell me about a lot of different cultures. "Oh well, Sasha says that her parents say this." "This is the way their family does this." And we can explain to them, that's a different culture and it's good to learn that and try different things and to be exposed to different things. So, all in all, I'm satisfied. I think the school system should be a little more diverse.

The interviewees did not always agree on the benefits of school integration. Kay Berry, who wanted "more residential integration," was skeptical about the benefits of school integration. "In school," she emphasized, "my sole concern with school is, is it topflight? Is the education something that would allow her [child] to fold into a Bethesda school district? I want her to get the exact same education as the best white kids, the best white kid schools, whether or not white kids are actually in it."

Those couples who praised the benefits of their children's exposure to other cultures most often spoke of culinary differences. One father with positive experiences growing up in an integrated environment recounted the equally positive experiences of his sons: "My boys have friends that are white, and they go visiting, and he talks about what they ate. Things have a different taste and they do things differently, so they understand; it's a learning thing." Another respondent spoke of her surprise when the daughter of a white neighbor ate several servings of a dish of collard greens she had prepared. She did not understand that whites might also enjoy this dish, which is so popular in the black community. My first impression was that these "discoveries" of culinary differences were superficial. With more reflection, though, I realized that food is such a part of our daily lives that differences in culinary tastes are important cultural markers. During the 1970s, when many whites discovered ethnicity, ethnic foods were important markers that appeared to buttress the claim of "unmeltable ethnics" by Robert Novak.[3] Sometimes racial contacts among the thirty-one couples I interviewed in Prince George's County went deeper. Such was the case with an exchange of visits by children of one black family and one Jewish family around the feasts of Christmas, Kwanzaa, and Hanukkah. Such interracial cultural exchanges seemed rare, however.

Over four decades, the largest African American middle-class suburb emerged in suburban Prince George's County. In part, new housing developments in the more rural and spacious area and the presence of significant numbers of blacks in the county appeared to have facilitated the development. As the numbers of middle-class African Americans migrating into the county increased, it seemed to have the potential of becoming a stable, diverse suburb by 1990. It was not to be. The familiar pattern of white flight in the face of black in-migration took hold. Court-ordered busing for school desegregation may have been the final push, leading to a predominantly black suburb that nevertheless retained some racially mixed neighborhoods. From the perspective of their lives often in predominantly affluent black middle-class neighborhoods, these couples had different opinions about racial integration. Some had no use for it, while others felt it was important for their children's future success. In the next chapter, I examine the feelings and attitudes of middle-class black couples about their communities. Had they found what they wanted, or were they disappointed?

4

Pick Up the Newspaper; We're Out of Town

In his 2001 book, *Bowling Alone: The Collapse and Revival of American Community*, Robert D. Putnam bemoaned the decline of community in the United States, using the decrease in the popularity of bowling as a metaphor for a larger national malaise.[1] The issue is important in understanding the emergence of the new black middle class in Prince George's County. What would the future bring for these new residents? Would communities develop, rather than just neighborhoods of impressive housing clusters?

When I interviewed the thirty-one couples in 2007, all but three had lived in their present home for five or more years; over half between eight and fifteen years, more than enough time to develop community. What are the ingredients of a community, in contrast to a neighborhood, and how does community really develop? What did these families want, and what did they find?

As I talked with these couples, several "ingredients" of community formation emerged: proximity, stability, time in the community, and friendliness. Proximity seems obvious. In urban areas, it is a truism that neighbors often do not know one another and never interact. Proximity, therefore, would appear to be a necessary but insufficient ingredient. When asked whom they knew, responses revealed the importance of proximity. "I know everybody on this strip. I know most of the people," James Douglas responded.

"Yeah, we know pretty much everybody," his wife, Mary, agreed. Jennifer Roberts also noted, "We know everybody in this cul-de-sac." The Edisons (only three years at their present address in Upper Marlboro) answered my question by counting fourteen families they knew and concluded, "It's mostly our street." Denise Brooks, also in Upper Marlboro, responded, "In the neighborhood? Probably five, five families. Know them enough to invite them over, spend time with them, go and sit in their houses, uninvited even."

Proximity—"on our street," "in the cul-de-sac"—is important in the formation of community. Other responses revealed other ingredients, such as time. Linda Tucker knew "almost everyone on this block, except someone who just moved in across the street. So, I would say maybe ten to fifteen families." Judy Harrington, whose family had lived in Mitchellville for fifteen years, used almost the same words when talking about the neighbors her family knew: "We know just about everybody in the neighborhood unless you just recently moved in."

While proximity and time seem to be necessary ingredients for community building, they are not sufficient. Something more is needed to bond with one's neighbors. That ingredient appears to be an atmosphere of friendliness and receptivity. Several couples, like the Harringtons, commented on these factors.

LANDRY: It's been easy to meet people?
JUDY: Yes.
PATRICK: People have been extremely friendly. One thing they do a
   lot in this neighborhood is just wave. And they do that just to,
   you know, just to see who you are. It's just one of those things.
   Everyone kind of waves at each other.

Interviewees often said, "I love my neighbors." Similarities functioned as a magnet that attracted people to one another and held them together. Susan and Darrell Snow spoke of going to the same church and having the "same interests" as their neighbors. Patrick Harrington emphasized, "It's a wonderful neighborhood. We all are pretty close. We're all like-minded people within this neighborhood." When pressed to define "like-minded," he described what many would consider an ideal community:

> We all care about a quality of life. We all look at a certain
> quality of life so we care about the way the community looks.
> We don't have many—there's always gonna be some bad
> apples—that don't absolutely take care of their property and take
> care of their yards. Everybody is pretty much on the same sheet.
> They want their homes and their yards to look as best as they
> possibly can. Nobody's really driving any big flashy cars. But
> I mean everybody's got nice cars. And that's the thing. There's
> no competition on trying to be better than anybody else. Well,
> for most. We just all go at the same pace. Because of that we're
> willing to share ideas and share thoughts, and we're happy when
> people do well and are not jealous. Shared happiness because
> somebody does well. You know, at least in the cul-de-sac. We
> know everybody else, but we're not as close to them as we are to
> the people in the cul-de-sac. And we're very close within this
> cul-de-sac, 'cause all but two families have been here since the
> beginning, and those two families that came in, came in and
> just joined the family. They've been accepted, and you know
> we're all like-minded and we help each other. When it snows,
> one guy got a snowblower; we take turns and we blow off
> everybody's driveway—that kind of thing. When the kids are
> out, I holler at all the kids. I don't care who they are, which
> house they came from; I'm gonna treat them just like I treat my
> own. And I think everybody appreciates that 'cause if they see
> me doing it, they don't say, "Stop."

There is little doubt that the similarities and friendliness underlining community development in these black middle-class neighborhoods were influenced by race. While most did not refer to race explicitly as an important ingredient of community building, the role of race came out in many statements, both directly and indirectly. Several couples who had lived in largely white, northern Virginia neighborhoods moved to Prince George's County because of the racial isolation they experienced previously. Rita Madison, who had lived in Alexandria, remembered the discomfort of being the only African American in stores there. This same couple had moved to Prince George's County to spare their daughter the stress of being a minority in classrooms in Alexandria. Kay and John Berry remarked that they knew "more [neighbors] here [in Prince George's County] than we did when we lived in Virginia." John spoke of "a comfort level" in their black neighborhood. "There's a translation you don't have to do. If your kids don't get along, they just don't get along. There's nothing; there's no overlay to it. There's nothing you have to parse out and figure out what it is and examine. You know, it's just the comfort that I sort of feel, but take for granted. But I feel it very keenly when I go out into the world and I don't have that, and it makes me recognize." Later in our conversation, Kay underscored the same idea when she said, "There's a power dynamic that I like here, that my education buys me, and my profession buys me, and my income buys me, that helps to equalize things. But when I go out in the world, you don't have that. I find myself, anytime I travel, even going back to Chicago, it's just a different weight, you know; my blackness weighs something different in another part of the country than it does here."

A Lot of Things in Common

Physical proximity, time in the neighborhood, and low turnover of residents have nurtured community building in the black middle-class neighborhoods of Prince George's County. Feelings of comfort derived from a sense of shared values and the absence of a need to negotiate meanings, "translate," or guess about underlining intentions or motives have also contributed to community building. Community, it would seem, develops when a set of conditions are present. Communities sometimes go beyond knowing one's neighbor and acknowledging them by waving. Greater depth develops when members make friends and socialize. Michael Jamison spoke of being able to just drop in on his neighbor across the street "and bother him." He added, "We know the folks around the corner, and they invite us to socials and things like that."

Speaking of her experience over her fifteen years living in Mitchellville, Judy Harrington explained her positive feelings: "I like the fact that it's predominately black. I mean that that's a plus for me. I like my neighbors a lot. And friends that we've made since we've been here are still our friends now. So we have a lot of things in common with the people that we associate with." As if to underscore this last statement, she added, "This past Saturday, we had a community yard sale. So we do a lot of things together. Especially this cul-de-sac. We call it the cul-de-sac. And we keep each other's kids. We go to each other's kids' graduations, parties, all ages. They're not all the same ages, but it's like a big family."

Acquaintances and Friends: It Really Wasn't a Neighborhood, It Was a Community

Some respondents distinguished between acquaintances and friends or struggled to define friendship. Herman Madison at first seemed to suggest that their relationships had not risen to the level of friendships, a suggestion later corrected by his wife.

LANDRY: How about your neighbors? Do you know your neighbors? Do you guys socialize?

HERMAN: We don't like to hang out, but we speak and everybody's pleasant. And if they go out of town, they'll ask us to get the paper, and we'll do the same. We'll talk while we're outside working in the yard, and that's about the extent of it.

RITA: Well, we have a couple that are a little bit closer than that. They come over and sit down, and we might share a drink or something, and they have young kids.

HERMAN: We let our kids play.

RITA: Yes. We have a couple that have expanded past that just neighborly pleasantry.

HERMAN: But it's not like the whole neighborhood is like, "Hey!"

RITA: Right.

HERMAN: Now the kids are all over the place. They're in everybody's house.

RITA: I think everybody is reciprocal of our neighbors, and there's been no issues and challenges that we've had.

Peggy Turner also distinguished between acquaintances and friends, replying there were "eight of what I consider close-knit. There are plenty of people you associate with but people you consider 'pick up the newspaper; we're out of town.'" It is interesting to note the different meanings attributed to picking up a neighbor's newspaper. While Peggy used the practice as a marker of friendship, Herman Madison viewed it as a sign of a more casual relationship. As my conversation with Rita and Herman continued, it seemed there was a certain amount of ambiguity in defining friendship.

LANDRY: So how many families do you know around here?

RITA: I know all the old ones, most of the old ones. But for me, it started with these houses here back this way, but not up that way. I know maybe all of them but one or two.

LANDRY: Do you have any friends there, or is it just sort of casual?

RITA: Well, if someone moves into the neighborhood, I try to go and introduce myself and speak and do something with them. Just to welcome them to the neighborhood. But that's usually about it.

LANDRY: What about the other ones that have been here for a while? Are you friends with any of them?

RITA: I wouldn't say we're friends, but we do mingle. Probably the two families across the street we do consider friends. But our neighbor next door, we don't know her that well, but we do talk.

HERMAN: What was it, a year and a half ago she moved in?

RITA: Something like that. We talk, and when she's leaving town, she'll call us, say watch my house. And I guess, yeah, we're friends.

HERMAN: Yeah, we're friends with Bertha and her husband. Her kids, as they were growing up, were playing with the kids across the street and the Crestwoods and the Whites, and so we'd even gone to Ocean City with them, so I'd say that's pretty good friendship. We put a basketball net out in front of the house. It drew a lot of kids; everybody was in our front yard.

As this dialogue suggests, children play an important role in influencing their parents' friendships. Since the children in many of these families had grown up, they often spoke of this early period in their family's history with a tinge of nostalgia.

LANDRY: Have you remained satisfied with the area?

RITA: Oh yeah. We have no complaints. I mean, the area's changed as the kids have grown up. They made lifelong friends who were like brothers here. And that is one thing about this development, that *it really wasn't a neighborhood; it was a community.* Everybody kind of knew everybody else's kids, and most of them were boys. So they were playing on this cul-de-sac, baseball or football. They had locations. And you kind of knew they were going to somebody's house, but they're usually in front of somebody's house doing some kind of sporting activity. So, in terms of raising our kids, I couldn't have wanted a better place.

In spite of the changes over time, this couple was still well entrenched in the community and knew a larger number of neighbors by name.

Exchange of Services

Friendships often lead to an exchange of services. This exchange of services is instrumental in binding a community closer together. In these communities, the services exchanged take many forms, and reciprocity creates a chain of actions. If I pick up your mail or newspaper when you are out of town, I feel free to ask for the same or some equivalent favor when I go away. We become more closely connected as a result. It is difficult to know the extent of the exchange of services in these black middle-class communities, but I found sufficient examples to believe it is widespread.

Beyond picking up a neighbor's newspaper, respondents talked about spontaneous groupings to reduce the cost of services, sharing, reciprocal help with childcare, and just "looking out" for each other. Patrick Harrington, whom I quoted above, spoke enthusiastically of his community's closeness by giving the example of sharing a snowblower. Peggy and Tony Turner described how neighbors exchanged useful information in their community.

TONY: As we talk to each other we literally go outside and somebody would say, "Hey, I'm gonna put something out on the grass to deal with this bug or fungus or worms or whatever. But it's gonna go your way, so you need to put yours down." And when people knew just from talking that we were finishing our basement, they called us and said, "This guy's doing the framing, even though I know you talked about you were going to wait; but it's such a good deal, it's somebody that I would recommend that did a good job, so come take a look." So it was already framed up and I told him, I said I need to find somebody to finish. He said you could do that yourself. I said not *me*! He said, you should do that. Let's do the bedroom, even if you don't want to do the rest, you'll learn what to look for. You'll know when someone tells you it's X amount of dollars, you'll know how much work that is. I did that, and it was a huge help.

LANDRY: So you all did the drywall?

TONY: Yeah, so we did the drywall. Electrical, the wiring.

PEGGY: One room.

TONY: Right. We're both full-time at the same place, and he said, "Come over for this weekend." And so while we were there, we were taught. It reminded me of seeing my older relatives and fathers and uncles at home, and they would just come on by. We're gonna do something. You're talking about everything— politics, relationships, things like that, and it was real. I really enjoyed it.

PEGGY: And that is one thing I feel like we do pretty decently, like even the sprinkler system for the lawn. There was one person putting in a sprinkler system. He offered a good deal. He actually gave us the volume discount. It works well.

TONY: He did thirteen homes in the area.

LANDRY: So what is it about this neighborhood? Are you still liking it?

TONY: What are the things I like about the neighborhood? It's small, you get a chance to meet. When you do know the people in the neighborhood, you find that most of them are friendly, most of them have kids, and the ones that we really communicate with are the families that have kids our [kids'] ages. When you communicate with them, you're talking about schools; you're talking about things for the kids to do. And that's our biggest thing that we wanted to make sure we find out the right things for kids to do, not only the school year but during the after school year too, summertime too.

How Structure Encourages Community

Beyond the human dimensions—proximity, shared values, exchange of services, and children—there are structural features in these neighborhoods that encourage contact with others. Most are planned and provide residents with a variety of amenities. Some have clubhouses with swimming pools. The majority have playgrounds, gazebos, and bike paths. Linda and Kevin Tucker expressed their satisfaction with these facilities, emphasizing how they helped connect neighbors and provide the family with convenient recreation.

LANDRY: What sort of things in the neighborhood connect people?

LINDA: You know, walking the dogs, and we all see each other on the bike paths.

LANDRY: You have a bike path?

LINDA: Yeah, there's a walking and bike path throughout the neighborhood.

KEVIN: They have all these common areas; they have these play-grounds and gazebos, picnic areas, and they have about three or four of them in the neighborhood.

LINDA: It's more than that. They have one here, two there, they're throughout.

KEVIN: They're all sort of linked along these paths. It's a good place to take your kids. That's one of the things that I fell in love with instantly. We had a son, and we had a daughter who was getting bigger. We just needed more space, and so that's one of the primary reasons that we were looking to move in the first place; but it's great that our kids can go out and can play.

Several respondents also met neighbors through meetings of their homeowners' association (HOA). Others cited attendance at the same church or having children in the same school. Community events like block parties also helped bind members more closely. It is these structural features and community events that, together with the human contacts mentioned earlier, seem to be the ingredients that encourage and shape the community. The result has been to tie families closely to their communities with which they identify. As Brenda White said, "Everyone identifies by neighborhood, by subdivision. 'I live in Perrywood, I live in Colington Station, I live in Woodmore Highlands.'"

Still, there were a few families who had not yet meshed with their neighbors. When asked about the people they knew, Arthur Smith answered, "We know folks, but we can't say that we're close with anybody." Then he added, somewhat regretfully, "I have friends who tell me, 'I was over at my neighbor's house watching the game.' Not that people aren't friendly. I just think it's a matter of time."

After interviewing the thirty-one families, it was clear that as neighborhoods grew over the past decades, communities had also emerged, resulting in a high level of satisfaction with life in these communities. A shared racial and class identity contributed to this development. Charles Brody expressed it by saying, "People, they're not naïve, but they're just not quite so guarded." A certain "comfort level" encouraged neighbors to reach out to one another, generating a friendliness that most people emphasized was present in their neighborhood. The structural arrangement of these planned neighborhoods also promoted meaningful contacts. I found out that my "acid test" of community, knowing and interacting with your neighbors, was widespread. In one community, even the failure to organize a homeowners' association resulted in a stronger community. This was the experience of Mary and James Douglas, who had wanted to organize an HOA when they first settled in their community in 1996. Although outvoted in their endeavor, they found a silver lining, the benefit of getting to "know people during that period." Mary noted, "In doing so [trying to organize an HOA] everybody got to know each other here and so we look out for each other. If I see anything happening around here, I'm gonna call; we have everybody's phone number. We call people."

In a society with a history of racial conflict, middle-class blacks appear to have created communities in the Washington, D.C., suburbs and presumably in other suburbs. Proximity, time, friendliness, comfort from similar racial identity and experiences, similar values, and exchange of services—all have contributed to general satisfaction with interviewees' residential choices. The absence of the need to negotiate meanings seem especially important to them. This is true in spite of the different attitudes toward racial integration discussed in the previous chapter. What seems most important in the end are the communities they were able to create. However, few communities are perfect. In the next chapter I explore the bigger picture of living in the Prince George's County suburbs. Although people live in communities, the larger level of the county is also important for life satisfaction. How are they served by the institutions of the county? Are their needs met? What are their reactions to these services?

5
Catch-22

The middle-class residents whom I interviewed had chosen Prince George's County for both financial and social reasons. That they could find more house for their money was important. For many more, it was the opportunity to live among "like-minded" neighbors, neighbors who were role models for their children, neighbors who would become members of their friendship circle. Prince George's County was a place where they would not have to worry about how they would be received, a place where they could relax among friends after a workday surrounded by whites. After living in Prince George's County for many years, few ever thought of moving to another county. They remained happy with their choice. It is important to emphasize this as we discuss areas of dissatisfaction on the county level.

One evening, as I sat at the dining room table of Jennifer and Troy Roberts until late into the night discussing the pros and cons of living in Prince George's County, it seemed to me that ironically the couple was trapped in a classic catch-22. How could that be? A beautiful home, friendly neighbors, a real community. They also had two children, ages seven and thirteen, both attending private schools.

This family is typical of the upper-middle-class black families who have settled in Prince George's County over the past three decades. Troy worked as a computer specialist, Jennifer as a senior systems analyst. Their first residence after marriage in 1990 was a rental apartment. Within four years, the pull of home ownership brought them to Mitchellville, where they bought a townhouse. Asked to explain their motives for choosing Prince George's County, they responded as many others had: more home for the money and the perception that "the county was growing." "We saw just talking to folks," Troy commented. "They were building, you know, friends that lived in Prince George's County. I don't know if I had too many friends in Montgomery County." Then there was the real estate agent selling Mitchellville as "a hot spot because Mitchellville [was] the up-and-coming premier place for blacks to live." Not even Troy's brother-in-law, who lived in nearby Montgomery County, could dissuade them from their choice.

The couple's next move six years later in 1997 took them to their dream house in another part of Bowie. Like other couples, each sought fantasy elements. For Troy, it was a three-car garage that was side-loaded. Jennifer explained his motivation: "He didn't want the three-car garages in the front of the house 'cause he felt it was 'let's make a deal,' door number one, door number two, door number three. So that was his requirement." Then she continued, "So my requirement was I wanted a large kitchen and a large bedroom." They also settled on what was less common in the county, a one-acre plot. At $300,000, they considered the house and property a bargain compared to prices in neighboring Montgomery County, where Jennifer emphasized they would have had to pay $50,000 to $75,000 more.

When I interviewed Jennifer and Troy in 2007, they were well established in a "close-knit" community. They knew everyone in their cul-de-sac, and as Troy added, "We know half of the ones in the circle going in at the other end. Quite a few people; probably 65, 75 percent of the people. Just homeowners' meetings and just riding past." What more could anyone ask for? A place of their own in a community they loved. Was this not the American Dream?

Despite all this, Jennifer confessed, "I don't know about my husband—he's very content—but I have contemplated moving." She continued with passion:

I do get a little annoyed with the lack of services and retail and things, that I still have to travel outside of the county to go shopping, or if I'm looking for something in particular, I already know based on the numerous times that I've shopped within the county, that I can't find what I'm looking for. And that does become quite annoying after so many times. You try to stay within, and spend your money here, and I'll be honest, I constantly go to Annapolis. *Constantly.* They built us a mall, this Bowie town center. It has absolutely nothing. They gave us a Macy's. They made the Macy okay, but it's still not anywhere near the higher-end stuff that they've put in the Macy in Annapolis. Or the size of it. They actually built that Macy and then added on to it. Instead of building it outright the size that's comparable to other Macy's in other counties. Because I guess they didn't think it would facilitate the support that they get from other locations. So it gets frustrating.

There was more. The family chafed at the need to send their sons, seven and thirteen, to private schools because of the under-performing school system in the county. Jennifer felt even more passionate about this. Again, repeating the temptation to move, she continued, "So there have been times that I have contemplated, maybe we should sell, maybe we should move. We actually have our children in private school because of the many issues that go on with scores in Prince George's County. So we're paying enor-mous taxes, but still spending money to send them to private school."

Troy joined in: "It's an embarrassment. You're in Prince George's County but you can't send your kids to public school." It was also clear that he was not as content as Jennifer suggested; but moving to Montgomery County, with its reputation for one of the best school systems in the country, raised other issues: "To move into Montgomery County and then not be accepted. I'm not saying that may not happen, but being that integrated, resi-dential integration you were talking about, we're all for it, but the folks we move beside may not be for it, and all of a sudden they got a for-sale sign in their yard. Of course, me being me, I'm gonna walk over there and say, 'Hopefully you're not moving because of me.'"

With the moving choice off the table, Jennifer showed signs of choosing the only other option should the school system improve. "Both of my kids have been in private school since they've been in kindergarten. I am tired of paying. My son is going into high school, and we are considering sending him to public high school because we have this new superintendent who is trying to make effective changes now."

Beneath all of this was their attachment to the community, which they loved and defended when colleagues at work questioned their decision to live in Prince George's County. Jennifer again spoke heatedly about her experience at work when colleagues learned that she lived in Bowie.

"Oh, you live in Prince George's County. How come you live out there?" I mean, they actually just say this kind of stuff out of their mouth. I'm like, what do you mean by that? "Oh, I heard that the school system's not too great there." That's the first thing they'll say. They don't talk about crime or anything like that; they always just target "I heard the school system's not too good out there." And I'm like, well you know, they're trying to improve it; it's a slow process. It's not gonna improve overnight, I said. But my kids are in private school. I actually make the sacrifice to pay for them to do that until the school system can get to where it needs to be with test scores and so forth. That's the answer that I pretty much give; but I enjoy living here. I enjoy all the friends again that we may know; we're a very close-knit community right here in our cul-de-sac and then beyond. So it's hard to give that up.

It seemed like being on the horns of a dilemma or a catch-22. On the one hand, they loved their community and enjoyed living in Bowie. On the other hand, they had to leave the county for services like shopping and restaurants and paid dearly to send their children to private schools. Considering they had bought the home of their dream for less than they would have had to pay in Montgomery County but had to pay a premium for private school tuition, I asked if their decision was "a wash." Jennifer responded immediately.

JENNIFER: No.

LANDRY: Financially?

JENNIFER: Financially—

TROY: Repeat that question again.

LANDRY: You have more house for your money here, but you've got to spend money on private school, rather than put them in public school; so the money you're paying, you save in the house, but you pay for the school. Is it a wash financially?

JENNIFER: I would say it's not. Again you have to look at the timeline. Is it a wash today? No. By no stretch of the imagination. I can't go to Montgomery County and get a home of this size and with the land for less than a million. I mean, honestly, we've looked. You can't get an acre lot without paying $970,000 plus. Okay, so what am I paying in private school, roughly $18,000 a year between the two schools. If I put that $18,000 back into our household, is it gonna allow me to afford a million dollar home? No.

TROY: Nope.

LANDRY: So you're still ahead?

JENNIFER: We feel we are. You know, we feel we are.

A large home with ample acreage and a comfortable community but poor services and schools is the bargain that the Robertses struck.

Another couple was more ambivalent about the bargain struck between house and school. Unlike Troy and Jennifer Roberts, who had two children in private schools, the Berrys had three children they were shuffling between public and private schools. They spoke long and passionately about their situation.

LANDRY: Well look, this seems like a trade-off; you can get more house for your money, but then you still gotta send your kids to private school, and you still pay taxes. Do you come out ahead financially?

KAY: I've had this conversation with just about every black professional with kids I know. There're two ways to do it. You live in the white neighborhood, send your kid to public school, but then you have to augment their environment with either church or Jack and Jill and social functions to get them a deliberate exposure to black folks because they're in a majority white environment. You have to shore them up in their blackness. You maybe don't get as much house, you certainly don't get this much land, you know; it's a trade-off, but you get to send them to public schools. Or you get to live in the black neighborhood where you have the exhale factor where, you know, okay, "Hey, how ya doin' folks?" All your neighbors look like you, you have that comfort level, your mainstream black folks, the doctor or whomever for your kids, but you can't send them to the schools.

LANDRY: Well, would you say that in the middle-class black neighborhood there's a catch-22?

KAY: Sure, absolutely.

JOHN: I think so. We're paying money into the private school, and it takes a certain amount of income to do that. So what happens is you spend more time working to produce the income, but then you have less time with your kids.

KAY: We work all the damn time.

JOHN: You have less time to spend with your children, at the same time provide the best education for them. To be honest with you, when we lived in Upper Marlboro, we were probably at peace living in that little small house because I was able to work when they took off and when Sandra was born, she [Kay] took off, and that was one of the most beautiful times, and she had a year to just spend with Sandra, had a whole year by herself. And the house wasn't huge, but it was a certain kind of peace around that, and now we're always kind of passing each other.

KAY: I'm like a computer with too many programs open, so I split memory in different programs. My job is higher profile. His job, he's climbed up the ladder, and we make over $200,000. But it doesn't feel like it because it goes out; it takes a lot to keep all this up.

JOHN: I call it our financial burn rate that is extremely high.

KAY: Our quality of life doesn't feel—

JOHN: The same.

KAY: I fantasize all the time about picking up. But I can't quite wrap my mind about moving south, although that's less expensive. So yeah, trade-offs, catch-22 all over the place, everywhere you look.

The School Dilemma

The bargain struck by Jennifer and Troy Roberts revealed two dilemmas that middle-class residents faced when choosing to live in Prince George's County, a county that had become a minority suburb: the dilemma of services, which included retail shopping and dining, and the dilemma of schooling. Most important was the dilemma presented by the public school system. This was by far the most critical because it threatened their ability to pass on their middle-class position to their children. These families were keenly aware of the importance of education for their children's futures, and it was part of their children's upbringing. The following exchange made this clear.

LANDRY: What are your aspirations for your kids in terms of how far you want them to go?

TROY: They know college is after high school, they do. 'Cause my son said I want this, I want that. Mom and dad just didn't buy this because it was easy getting; we had to *buy* this. We didn't get just any kind of job, you have to go to college and focus on a career that you want and then come out and still work hard to get the job that you want.

LANDRY: You're telling them that?

TROY: Yeah, I'm telling them this. You want to be happy at whatever you do, but you got to have the job that's going to provide what you want to do in life. And if you don't go to college, there's no other way you can get it.

JENNIFER: So in short, Mr. Landry, my children know, and even my soon to be second grader, there are no options. And I have said this verbatim; there are no options because my dad didn't give me one. I had no option when I finished high school, there was no option. It wasn't even up for discussion. And that's what I'm telling them.

Kay Berry emphasized the historical depth of this conviction when she commented, "Since we're people who only got here through education, that was the thing that we had drilled in our head, whether you were working-class or not. We used to be of one accord, and it was education, get your education. The bum on the street could tell me to get my education."

If the route to a college education is solid preparation in well-performing schools, then the school system has been the Achilles' heel of Prince George's County and of the black suburban community there. Among the surrounding counties in Maryland, only Baltimore County's schools have ranked lower than Prince George's, as measured by the Maryland State Performance Assessment Program (MSPAP).

PRINCE GEORGE'S COUNTY SCHOOL SYSTEM

In chapter 3, I briefly discussed the effect of court-ordered busing for school desegregation and its effect on white flight. Here I want to discuss Prince George's School system as an institution that has impacted the quality of life of middle-class African American residents and their educational aspirations for their children. Young black couples who moved into Prince George's County were generally unaware of the turbulent history of the county's school system. Not until they had school-aged children did the full force of the underperforming system begin to impact their lives. With two and three school-aged children, respectively, the Roberts and Berry families represent the frustrations of the middle-class couples who faced the challenge of the school system's failure.

The failure of the school system antedated the migration of most middle-class black couples into the county by several decades and was exacerbated by school segregation. It was first a problem of inferior education for black students under the separate-but-equal doctrine. Later, during and after the period of court-ordered busing for school desegregation, it became the problem of under-performing schools. The first issue was addressed in 1972 when the NAACP challenged racial segregation in the schools on behalf of eight African American families, arguing that Prince George's dual racial system provided African American children with an inferior education. A federal court responded by ordering busing to desegregate the school system. According to the court order, schools were to have no more than 50 percent and no less than 10 percent black students. The result would be integrated schools that would have the resources that the all-black and predominantly black schools lacked. In theory, black students would then receive the same quality schooling as whites. During this period, other school systems around the country embarked on similar busing programs by order of the courts; but Prince George's County was the only school system in the Washington, D.C., metropolitan area so affected. The order was issued in a turbulent period in the history of Prince George's school system that would span almost thirty years.

Court-ordered busing seemed like a great idea. It did not work out as planned. In 1973, 80 percent of students in the system were white, following the racial demography of a county that was 85 percent white. When busing began in January 1973, forty-six schools had black majorities. Four years later, eighty-five schools had black majorities, primarily in areas of high black concentration inside the beltway. As in other cities that introduced court-ordered busing, hordes of white families either left the county or transferred their children to private schools.

In the year following the start of busing, the white student population declined by 9.4 percent. In varying degrees, the exit continued each year following. By the end of the decade, white student enrollment had declined by 41 percent. The in-migration of black families, which began in the 1960s, accelerated during the 1970s, bringing in almost as many blacks (156,000) as whites (170,000) who moved out. The influx of African American families increased black student enrollment by 45 percent, while the black population itself expanded from 14 percent in 1970 to 37 percent in 1980. Since the school boundaries established in response to the court order remained in place while demographic changes quickened, several unintended consequences occurred. One was a trend toward resegregation resulting from white flight in areas involved in busing. At first, an equal number of black and white students were bused. By the late 1980s, about 80 percent of bused students were black. Some black students were shuttled to formerly majority-white schools that were now majority black. This continued even though the court changed the racial guidelines, from a maximum of 50 percent black students to a maximum of 80 percent.

There were three geographic areas, each with different attitudes about busing. The area of mainly working-class black concentration inside the beltway and close to the District of Columbia was the first. Most of the busing between mostly black and nearby largely white schools occurred in this area. It was also these nearby white areas that emptied of white families who wanted to avoid busing. The second geographic area was a "middle ring of the county" outside the beltway. Here, some residential integration occurred as middle-class black families entered. By the end of 1979, parts of this area had become 50 percent black. Yet busing from this formerly white area continued, even though now 60 percent of the children being bused were black. The third area outside the beltway and farther north was largely white and too distant for busing given the court's thirty-five-minute limit.[1]

Against this background, the virtually all-white school board (except for one black member) discussed ways to reduce busing and return many students to neighborhood schools, primarily in the "middle ring." Newly arrived middle-class black families were supportive of this initiative. Van Gilmer, a black architect who served as vice president of the Riverbend Homeowners' Association, voiced the association's sentiment. "When we moved into the neighborhood we saw the schools and thought they would be for our children. The system is doing it to us again: my children are being forced into a segregated environment [by busing]."[2] Support for an end to busing in the middle ring also came from a new group of middle-class black parents, the Black Coalition against Unnecessary Busing. James Garrett, the group's chairman, spoke for the group in an interview: "Prince George's now is one of the most integrated counties in the United States, and we want to keep it that way. But you're not going to do that with busing. Let's face reality. You can't really mandate that you'll have whites in the schools. And I'm not willing to have my children chase them all the way to Charles County or Virginia just to sit next to them in the classroom."[3]

In contrast to the increasing integration of the middle ring, schools inside the beltway, where 64 percent of the county's black population resided, continued to have mostly black student bodies. These schools had an average of 74 percent black students, with eleven exceeding 80 percent.[4] Although newspaper accounts did not focus on class differences, it stands out here. A large percentage of African American families inside the beltway were working-class, and their children had long suffered from the inferior resources received by the schools they attended. Their attitudes about busing were more mixed, given the history of the dual education system they had suffered. There was, on the one hand, the opinion that black students would profit from school integration because with more whites in school their children would not "get cheated out of anything."[5] Another parent was quoted as saying, "From an integrated environment everybody gets out of the starting blocks at the same time. Coming from a completely black environment, a kid might be a little more reluctant to approach a white boss or a white co-worker."[6] Claiming a second position, as reporter Lynn Wynter noted, were parents interested in "more resources, not additional white students."[7] One of these parents emphasized, "It won't matter if they bus in or out. But I think they need more programs to help learning ability." The introduction of magnet and Milliken II schools (named after the *Milliken v. Bradley* school desegregation suit) offered more opportunities but failed to solve the general problem of academic quality in the schools. The impasse forced parents to choose between public and private schools.

SCHOOL QUALITY AND THE PUBLIC OR PRIVATE SCHOOL CHOICE

Improving the quality of the school system has been daunting. Among the most important challenges have been adequate funding and administration stability. To address school quality, Maryland's governor and General Assembly created the Commission on Education Finance, Equity, and Excellence in 1999. The recommendations of the Thornton Commission (named after its chairman, Dr. Alvin Thornton, a former member of the school board) were passed by the state legislature three years later. The increased funding that followed enabled many improvements, including allowing the system to attract more qualified teachers and to lower the teacher-to-student ratios. Unfortunately, the recession of 2008 led to a decline in overall educational funding. Amid these continuing efforts to improve educational quality, parents struggled to find quality schooling for their children.

The nine couples who moved to Prince George's County between 1979 and 1989 had the longest experience of all interviewees with the school system. While probably not aware of it, they moved in when the Prince George's County suburb was transitioning from a largely white to an integrated suburb. Busing had existed for a decade or more. They witnessed at eye level white flight from some areas of the county and from the schools. They first settled in apartments or townhouses inside the beltway or the "middle ring," where most of the busing was occurring. As they had children, these young couples needed to choose between sending their children to public or private schools. Of these nine couples, only two sent their children exclusively to public schools and one to only private schools. The other seven used a combination of public and private schools. When moving to the county, they had thought little about the school system. Their goals had been to maximize their housing budget and to find a community of like-minded middle-class African Americans. Once settled, they eventually realized that despite finding their dream community, there were problems to confront. The experience of the Bells, who moved from Boston in 1989, represented many in this group. When asked why they had come to Prince George's County, Julia replied that unlike Boston, where the black middle class was "fragmented" and without "a sense of community," they found a sense of community here. Then she added, "Of course we came here and we found out that the school system had some serious challenges."

James and Mary Douglas, who had moved from Alexandria, Virginia, also echoed this contrast between a county they liked and a school system that failed to meet their children's needs. Mary emphasized that she had "not regretted" the move to Prince George's County "other than the school system, which we ended up putting our son in private school." The family had started their son in public school and then transferred him to a private school. "After a couple of years," Mary continued, "we needed to put him somewhere else. So that's disappointing. That's disappointing, but the county itself, if it wasn't for the declining school system, I think it's really, it's really a nice county and a nice place to live."

The Harrisons spoke angrily about the need to transfer their son to private school at a great financial cost.

FRANK: The schools are not great.
JOYCE: I hate P.G. County public schools. Because in my son's class, I think there were thirty people. And he needs a little help. He has fallen in some areas through the cracks.

To make it clear that her anger was directed toward the school system rather than specific teachers, she added, "And I know that the teachers can't do everything. I'm not faulting the teachers. I'm sure that they do the best that they can."

Still, the consequences were the same.

JOYCE: So this year coming up is going to be his last year in public school. He's going to be going into the eighth grade. And so I told him, if his grades get up then we'll try to either put him in DeMatha or in the Queen Anne's school. Now the Queen Anne's school is an arm and a leg.

FRANK: $18,000 a year.

JOYCE: Now, if he shows some promise, I'll sacrifice and live on $18,000 a year less. As long as he's not in school playing. Because I know he needs a smaller class.

The twenty-one African American middle-class families who settled in Prince George's County during the 1990s and 2000s faced the turmoil discussed above and made different choices for their children's schooling. In 2007 when I interviewed them, nine families were using only private schools. Six had all their children in public schools, and six were using both public and private schools. I will discuss these choices in chapter 9.

The Service Dilemma: Shopping

Gaining excellent schooling for their children presented the primary dilemma for African American middle-class couples. The absence of upscale shopping and restaurants was also very frustrating to most. Our discussion on shopping generated the most heat. These were college-educated individuals who worked very hard to advance in their respective careers and by any measure were successful. Living in affluent communities, they compared the services available to them with services in neighboring counties. The comparisons left most frustrated, chagrined, and even angry. As the county's reputation as a large, affluent, African American community grew regionally and nationally, they expected that upscale businesses would seek this new market. This was not happening.

There have been four malls in Prince George's County: Prince George's Plaza, Capital Plaza Mall, Landover Mall, and Bowie Town Center. Prince George's Plaza opened in 1959 as an open-air mall and was enclosed in the late 1970s. Only one of the couples I interviewed mentioned it, perhaps because it lies well inside the beltway, far from their residences. Likewise, the mall's three major anchors, Macy's, JCPenney, and Target, hardly provide the upscale shopping lacking in the county. Capital Plaza Mall opened in 1963 with great fanfare that included representatives from foreign countries, but eventually it fell on bad times after the more popular Landover Mall opened in 1972. Denise Brooks referred to the sad state of shopping in the county: "When Landover Mall first opened, it was the mall to go to for the entire D.C. metropolitan area. It was new. It was two stories inside. And you know slowly but surely it deteriorated." As the neighborhood changed, many of the anchor stores departed, and the mall closed in 2002. Bowie Town Center, an open-air mall, did not open until 2000. Today it is anchored by Macy's, Sears, Barnes and Noble, Bed Bath & Beyond, and Old Navy.

Couples often criticized Bowie Town Center. To some, the open-air design of the mall itself was proof that Bowie Town Center was not really a mall like covered malls in neighboring counties. Jerry Brooks summarized his opinion about the mall: "Bowie Town Center is an outdoor mall. I don't know why P.G. County can't have a mall like Annapolis Mall or an indoor mall, instead of having everything outside. You get everything from outside. Bowie Town Center was a center, I think, they just threw up because they knew we're out here, and out here, we're gonna go there anyway. And try to keep us here. No really name-brand stores here; the only store in Bowie Town Center that's name brand, if you want to call it, is Macy's. So there are no really name-brand stores in Bowie Town Center."

"We don't have a mall here" was the flat assertion of Patrick Harrington. "You know, we don't have a mall so we don't have those little boutiques you know like the Oakley Store. The nicer sports stores other than tennis shoe stores, you know. Small boutiques, that specialize in different things."

The Bowie Town Center's Macy's received even harsher criticism. Although some saw it as a kind of higher-end store, many more found it lacking. Brenda White commented,

> There's a Macy's there now [in Bowie Town Center], but I think over the years they've changed their lines. Because when they first came in, all they carried were jogging suits and sweatpants and t-shirts. We used to ask, is this a warehouse or wholesale Macy's? Well, it was Hecht's [a previous company acquired by Macy's]. Well, what type of Hecht's are you? Is this the outlet Hecht's, or are you regular? And I think it's taken people in the neighborhood to say, no, we have jobs and we have to wear suits. And we don't want sweatpants and t-shirts. We need better lines, and they have those lines in other stores. But if I want to buy a suit I can't buy a suit. I have to go to another county, I have to go to Anne Arundel, to go to Annapolis Mall or I have to go to Pentagon City. I can't go anywhere [here] and buy a business suit.

The harshest criticism came from women who compared the Macy's in the Bowie mall to Kmart. "I was there [Annapolis Mall] yesterday," Julia Bell complained, "to get some cosmetics I can't find at Bowie Town Center. That Macy's [in Bowie Mall] is more like a Kmart. It is. You go to Macy's at Pentagon Center and you go to Macy's at Bowie, and the buyers don't buy the same kind of clothes. They're substandard. But if you go to the one at Pentagon City, the quality of the merchandise is much better. I've said that for years even about grocery stores. You go to a white neighborhood to get fresher food. And I was hearing that in high school."

These harsh criticisms and complaints revealed the depth of frustration felt by many couples over the lack of shopping similar to neighboring counties. Nordstrom was most often mentioned as the store these couples wanted in the county. Other desirable stores mentioned included Ann Taylor, Saks, and Whole Foods Market.

When I asked the reason for the lack of upscale shopping, I received various answers. Judy Harrington responded, "I don't know what the answer is. I'm just thinking that maybe some of the businesses think it's maybe a risk. I don't know the real reason for why we don't have it." Several others voiced their suspicion of racism. Linda Tucker was firm in her view: "Because it's a large African American county, honestly." At greater length, Jennifer Roberts also expressed the same conviction: "Because we're 85 percent black, to be honest with you, and that's the real truth. Again, because we still live in quote-unquote white America, they still see us as inferior, as an inferior class overall. Now granted I think to some extent they acknowledge communities such as Mitchellville and Bowie and places like that, where the average household income is probably six figures, combined income sometimes. But they still don't want to recognize us having a slice of what the other counties should enjoy."

While most couples were very dissatisfied with the shopping in Prince George's County, there were a few who liked Macy's or at least gave it a pass. This was true of Denise Brooks, who confessed to liking the Macy's in Bowie Town Center, although she also said of the Nordstrom in Annapolis, "I love that one."

Marlene George also felt positive about both the mall and Macy's.

LANDRY: What do you think of that Macy's?
MARLENE: I think it's a pretty decent store. I should say I was kind of surprised because I didn't know what things were gonna be like here. Sometimes a store's different than a store in like a Gaithersburg store, Tysons Corner store, something like that. I really haven't been disappointed with Bowie Town Center, and I actually kind of like when we went there. When it first opened, they had a whole little parade down Main Street. And one of the things I actually like about Bowie is it sometimes has

a small-town feel but then other times, it has a—it never has a city feel to me—a more suburban feel.

A few couples either confessed to not being "big shoppers" or cited financial considerations for their support of Macy's. This was true of the Edisons.

LANDRY: Where do you shop?
THOMAS: We're not big shoppers.
SHIRLEY: I shop on the internet.
LANDRY: You're not looking for the high-end stores?
SHIRLEY: No.
THOMAS: No.
SHIRLEY: You gotta pay the high-end money.
LANDRY: You go to Bowie Town Center?
SHIRLEY: I have.
THOMAS: But most of the time, what we are doing there, something for the kids, music, shoes, bookstores. It's kind of that the kids used to go to school in Bowie, 'cause they're in the magnet program, the tag programs [talented and gifted], so they were being sent to Bowie originally. So that's kind of how we got the tie-in to the Bowie area. And now, I know where everything is, and it's just straight up the highway. Like we said, creature of habit. It's more so that than anything else because if I want to buy clothes, we get them when we go to North Carolina. That's bargain hunter's delight.

Margaret Francis referred to her "practical side" and cited having three children as determinants of her shopping choices.

LANDRY: Where do you shop?
MARGARET: You mean clothing-wise or food?
LANDRY: Clothing.
MARGARET: To be honest, because I have three children I shop Target. I call it *Tar-jeh*. That's me, though, because some of my friends they like the Nordstrom's. I like to look nice and do

things, but there's a practical side of me. And I just refuse to spend. Sometimes I would like to have high-end stores because I think we don't have enough of those. And I think we don't have enough nice restaurants as well. I don't like all the Applebee's and the Fridays. And we go out of the area! Which is fine. It's nice to get away. So I don't like that we don't have some upscale restaurants. I don't too much mind the clothing part. I like Target a lot 'cause you got a little bit of everything; but I don't have to shop at Nordstrom.

LANDRY: Macy's?

MARGARET: I go to Macy's sometimes.

The Service Dilemma: Dining

Middle-class couples in Prince George's County complained about the lack of "fine dining" or "white tablecloth" restaurants. The following exchange is a good example of the conversations I had on this subject. The Brodys made distinctions between wanting to "dine instead of just eating out" and—as most couples did— between chain restaurants and "white tablecloth" restaurants.

LANDRY: What about restaurants? I know you've got kids, so I don't know what the kids like. But for yourself, when you want to go out, just the two of you, do you find restaurants?

CHARLES: Actually, most of the time when we decide to go out we go into the city. Something like B. Smith's.

ROSE: But when we do the family, we hit TGI Fridays.

CHARLES: Or Carrabba's Italian Grill.

ROSE: Carrabba's. Longhorn, Smokey Bones.

LANDRY: In the city?

CHARLES: No. They're right out here. But if you want something in the city—

ROSE: We want to dine instead of just eating out.

LANDRY: You go to the city?

ROSE: Yeah. It's a special occasion for us.

LANDRY: So there's not really any places where you would dine.

ROSE: There was one upscale bistro called Strawberry's in Bowie Town Center, and people sort of exhaled and said, "Ah, ha. Finally someplace upscale." And they had a little jazz area. And I can recall it was the year that we had the large snow, and the profit margin for restaurants is very small. And we had just weeks upon weeks of bad weather. And they were just, I guess, undercapitalized.

ROSE: But in terms of white tablecloth atmosphere, in this particular area we just don't have that yet.

Although it was more important to some couples, almost all acknowledged that it was necessary to go to other counties for fine dining. In a large metropolitan area like the Baltimore-Washington metropolis, this could entail a thirty-minute drive or more. Brad Hamilton complained, "There are enough Fridays. We've got that. You do those things with the children. But we're talking about white tablecloth occasions; why do you have to drive forty or fifty minutes?" The Georges, who called themselves "homebodies," confessed to not knowing where to go in Prince George's County if they wanted to dine out. Roy Bell observed in a matter-of-fact tone, "In major upscale restaurants, there's nothing like that here." Tony Turner was more forceful: "There's just absolutely nothing in the county of any stature."

Even Margaret and Stephen Francis, who eschewed high-end shopping because they had three children, were frustrated by the lack of "upscale restaurants" and noted that they had to go to neighboring counties to celebrate special occasions like birthdays. The Whites faced the dilemma of how to support their community in the face of the absence of upscale restaurants.

LANDRY: Do you go to restaurants much?
ANDREW: Yes, we do.
LANDRY: Where do you go?
BRENDA: On special occasions, we'll go to D.C. And there're a couple of restaurants that we like in Virginia. In Annapolis. But I'm kind of a firm believer and I like to support my community,

and I like to put my dollars where they benefit me. All things being equal—quality, service, price—I prefer to support things in my community.

LANDRY: So do you find some restaurants that you are pleased with?

BRENDA: Yes.

ANDREW: There are some pretty good restaurants locally. There are no, I would say, upscale restaurants.

BRENDA: Right. That's missing.

ANDREW: Like when I want to have a really nice, quiet dinner with my wife where we just sit down and not be rushed out. I don't have much of that here.

While there was widespread dissatisfaction over the lack of fine dining, a few couples said that they did not "eat out often." Claudia Gilbert explained their habit by saying, "We go out to eat; we don't go out to eat enough to call for any upscale restaurants, you know." Peggy Turner confessed, "I'm not really big into exclusive restaurants."

At the time of my interviews, a new multipurpose development of shops, restaurants, hotels, and entertainment was being built on the Potomac River in Prince George's County. This new development was to be called National Harbor. Expectations among the couples varied, with some prepared to explore its offerings once it opened and others deterred by the distance from Bowie.

People live their lives at multiple levels: neighborhood, county or city, and even metropolitan area. Each provides resources that together constitute a potentially rich and satisfying lifestyle. Chapter 2 traced the migration that eventually created the black upper-middle-class suburban neighborhoods of Prince George's County. In chapter 3, I explored the impact of race on the composition of these neighborhoods. On the county level, the racial/ethnic mix went through major changes, from predominantly white to a period of diversity, and finally to predominantly black. At the base of these changes was the familiar white flight that often accompanies the in-migration of African Americans. At the same time, neighborhood racial/ethnic compositions varied from all black to some degree of diversity. The response of black families to these changes varied, but in general, most were concerned less with integration than with living in comfortable, and supportive, black communities. Chapter 4 examined the degree of satisfaction these middle-class suburban couples found in their neighborhoods. It was clear that they were very happy with their choice to settle in these black upper-middle-class communities, because of the comfort they found among like-minded neighbors. Chapter 5 rounded out my examination of these black middle-class communities by focusing on their attitudes toward the services received on the county level. The assertion by Orfield and Luce that diverse suburbs provide the best services was borne out. In spite of their level of satisfaction with their communities, black middle-class families struggle with an underperforming school system compared to the schools in surrounding predominantly white or diverse counties. They likewise found upscale shopping and dining wanting.

In the next chapters, I explore the routes taken to become a member of the upper middle class. Both the process of attainment and the elements of this process are examined.

6

Educating the New Black Middle Class

Education is viewed as the escalator to success in the United States. Millions of immigrants who arrived in the nineteenth century and those who continued the trek, legally or illegally, in the twentieth and twenty-first centuries have pinned their hopes on education, if not for themselves then for their children. African Americans have long considered education not only as the key to upward mobility but also as the surest escape from racism and discrimination. As Kay Berry emphasized in the previous chapter, "Since we're people who only got here through education, that was the thing that we had drilled in our head, whether you were working-class or not. We used to be of one accord, and it was education, get your education." This belief has continued among blacks, even though education has been a porous shield against discrimination. Why, then, this unshakable faith in educational attainment as the route to a better life? It is because there is a general understanding of the connection between education and occupation and therefore between education and upward mobility.

Education and Upward Mobility

When people think of upward mobility, most envision movement into the middle class. Americans believe that, apart from the rich, the *good life* is in the middle class, especially in the upper middle class. In the previous chapter, we saw how Troy Roberts, who understood the connection between education and occupation from his own experience, emphasized to his son: "You have to go to college and focus on a career that you want." Their struggles to obtain quality primary and secondary education for their children led them to private schools but did not stop there. The next step was "sponsoring" their children's entrance into college so they could earn a college degree.

Is this belief in education and the connection between education and upward mobility warranted by the facts? How tight is this connection, and is it the same for all groups? To answer these questions, we must digress for a brief discussion on class. The most widely held view among sociologists is that occupation is the best measure of class position. This belief follows the sociologist Max Weber who, along with Karl Marx, provided the most compelling approach to class analysis. Marx and Weber agreed that the major class cleavage runs along the fault line between the very wealthy who own the lion's share of financial, industrial, and real estate assets and those who have to punch a real or figurative time clock most days of the year to survive. Owners versus workers. Beyond this point, Marx and Weber differed significantly. Marx gave scant attention to white-collar workers, believing they would eventually be trampled under the feet of the capitalist, as nineteenth-century manual laborers were. Weber, who wrote in the late nineteenth and early twentieth centuries, saw firsthand that white-collar workers were not only different from the downtrodden factory workers of the day but that their numbers were increasing as businesses moved from small owner-managed enterprises to large corporations.

The *contrast* between oppressed factory workers who toiled in dangerous conditions for low wages with no recourse to unions or collective bargaining and white-collar workers who enjoyed the clean environments of corporate offices was salient to nineteenth- and early-twentieth-century Americans. This was a class divide among workers that was all too visible in everyday life, in the clothes people wore, the homes and apartments they lived in, and the recreational places they frequented. From this vantage point it is easy to understand the terms "working class" and "middle class," the first being manual workers, later called blue-collar workers, and the second nonmanual or white-collar workers. Above both were the owners of factories and the increasingly large corporations.

Since the early twentieth century, the economy has become more complex and more diversified, with fewer industrial workers and more people employed in white-collar service jobs. Yet the division remains. It is a division between those who are more vulnerable—with less secure jobs, lower pay and benefits, and fewer chances for upward mobility—and those who are more secure, receive higher pay and benefits, and often find opportunities for upward mobility. The intense competition of globalization and periods of economic downturn threaten all workers to some extent. Nevertheless, the life chances of white-collar workers are better. For this reason, the middle class is the desired destination. There is a great deal of difference between working-class and middle-class occupations, in skill level, pay, rank, and opportunities for upward mobility. On average, nonmanual (service) workers have the edge, and sometimes that edge is a large gulf. The sociologist C. Wright Mills wrote about this group in a classic study, *White Collar: The American Middle Classes* (1951).[1] A few years later William H. Whyte produced his iconic book about managers and executives, *The Organization Man* (1956).[2] Both books were critical studies of the middle class as it was growing at mid-century.

Max Weber recognized the difference between the middle and working classes and noted that individuals traded their skill set for a position in the labor market. The higher the skill level, the higher the position on the occupational ladder. The language has changed today, and we are more likely to talk about education than skill. Today we can think of the middle class as composed of workers with nonmanual jobs or white-collar occupations. There is a further division among nonmanual workers between those occupying the most favorable positions of professionals and managers or executives and those we call technical, sales, and clerical workers. This is the division between the upper middle and lower middle class. In the language of class analysis, they constitute two *strata* of the middle class. A place in the upper-middle-class stratum is most sought after, and it is to gain entrance into the upper stratum that students spend long years in classrooms on college campuses. This is why, as we saw, Troy and Jennifer Roberts were preparing their children for college; because it is only by earning a college degree that the children can "reproduce" the middle-class position of their parents.

Returning to the question of the connection between education and upward mobility leads us to a considerable body of sociological research that has modeled the attainment process.[3] The model posits a *three-stage* process beginning in the family, progressing through the educational system, and ending in the labor force. At the start, the family uses its resources (economic, educational, cultural, and social) to "sponsor" their children through their journey. At the end of the second stage, the children emerge with the skills and credentials they have earned. With diploma in hand, they enter the third stage to claim a personal place in the class system. No longer is their class position a reflection of their parents'; they now claim their own class position, whether it is that of a clerk, doctor, mechanic, butcher, baker, or candlestick maker.

Family ⟶ Education ⟶ Labor Force

Is this process the same for all groups? In its broadest outline, yes. Everyone must negotiate the three stages. Yet research has found that at all three stages in the process, gender, race, and ethnicity play important roles as resource or impediment.[4] Women earn 72 percent of men's salaries and face a daunting glass ceiling in their upward mobility. Many black and Latino children attend inferior neighborhood schools and face discrimination both when entering and moving through the job market. As we have seen in previous chapters, even in black middle-class communities children may face considerable obstacles. The connection between education and class attainment is real but operates always under the influence of gender, race, and ethnicity. The growth of the African American middle class is, therefore, strongly tied to progress in negotiating obstacles encountered along the journey to a college education.

College Education: From the Civil Rights Movement to the Present

The black middle class has grown since the civil rights movement and the Civil Rights Act of 1964. This progress is best understood in comparison with the gains of non-Hispanic whites. In 1964 only 3.9 percent of African American males and females, 25 years and older, held a bachelor's or higher degree, compared to 9.6 percent of whites. These low figures reflect the negative effect of discrimination on black educational attainment and, for both blacks and whites, the state of higher education and the economy in 1964. As late as the end of the Second World War, 38 percent of non-farmworkers were in manufacturing and only 10 percent in white-collar service industries. By 1964, the manufacturing sector still led the service sector. The above college attainment figures also reflect the slow development of our higher education system.

In the decades following 1964, buoyed by desegregation of universities and colleges in the South, the percentages of blacks earning bachelor's and higher degrees increased significantly— from 3.9 percent in 1964 to 19.9 percent in 2011. Still the attainment of whites was much higher, rising from 9.6 percent in 1964 to 31 percent in 2011, a gap of 11.1 percentage points. Desegregation in higher education and affirmative action had helped blacks gain higher degrees but not enough to keep up with the surge among whites.

Perhaps the lower attainment figures for African Americans 25 years and older reflect the still high percentage in this group of those generations who lived during the period of segregation when southern colleges and universities were closed to blacks. To check this assumption, I turned to a younger age group (25–29 years) that excludes those older generations. (See Figure 6.1.) In 1964, a slightly higher percentage of blacks in the 25–29 age group

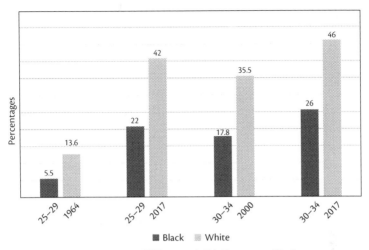

Black ■   White ░

FIG. 6.1. Percentage Black and White with BA Degrees or Higher
Source: Author's calculations based on CPS Historical Time Series Table A-2
and U.S. Census Data, Educational Attainment in the United States Table 1.

had earned a bachelor's degree or higher (5.5 percent compared to
3.9 percent). The percentage for whites 25–29 years was 13.6 percent.
By 2011, the percentage of blacks 25–29 years with a bachelor's
degree or higher had risen by only 14.1 percentage points to
19.6 percent, almost identical to the percentage of the 25+group
(19.9 percent). By comparison, 39 percent of whites in the 25–29
cohort had earned a bachelor's degree or higher by 2011. This gap
between blacks and whites 25–29 was *larger* (by 19.4 percentage
points) than the 11.1 percentage points between the 25+racial
groups. The lower percentage of college-educated blacks is not
reflective of older generations in the 25 years or older group. The
process of college attainment still favors whites, even among
those in the youngest age cohort.

Could it be, though, that the 25–29 year cohort is too young to
reflect total gains by blacks in college attainment? Perhaps there
is a delay in educational attainment that is not reflected in the
younger cohort. What do we find if we examine the attainment of
those in the 30–34 years cohort? These statistics are only available
from 2000. In 2000, 17.8 percent of blacks 30–34 years had earned
a bachelor's degree or higher, about the same percentage as the

25–29 and 25+ groups. After 2000, the 30–34 years group fared somewhat better than the other two age groups. In 2017, 26 percent of blacks in the 30–34 years cohort had a bachelor's degree or higher compared to 22 percent of the 25–29 years group. Still, the attainment of the 30–34 age group of blacks pales in comparison to that of whites, whose percentage in 2017 was almost twice (46 percent) that of blacks.

What can we conclude from these statistics? First, blacks have indeed made progress since 1964 in gaining the credentials needed for upper-middle-class professional and managerial jobs. This has fueled the growth of the black middle class. Second, a large racial education gap remains even among the youngest cohorts. There is one more interesting finding in these statistics. When we compare the percentage of blacks and whites with "some college" to the percentage with a bachelor's degree or higher, we find *opposite patterns*. (See Figure 6.2.) I should point out that "some college" includes those who entered college but failed to earn a bachelor's degree and those who have earned an occupational or academic two-year associate's degree. These last two groups represent about 8 to 10 percent of the "some college" group among both blacks and whites. The majority of the "some college" group are those who entered but did not obtain a bachelor's degree. What are the respective proportions of these two groups among blacks and whites, and what do we learn from this?

In 2017, among the 30–34 year cohort, there was about 26 percent of blacks with a bachelor's degree or higher, compared to 38 percent with some college. The proportions were the opposite among whites, who had a higher percentage with a bachelor's degree (46 percent) than with only some college (27 percent). How can we explain these different racial patterns? They suggest the greater difficulty black students have in reaching the top of the educational ladder. In this 30–34 years cohort, there are more blacks than whites who have not finished high school (8 percent to 4 percent), more blacks with only a high school diploma (28 percent to 23 percent), and more with just some college (38 percent to 27 percent). The cumulative deficits appear as a lower percentage

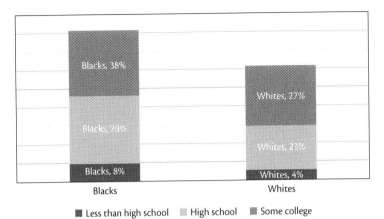

Blacks, 38%

Whites, 27%

Blacks, 23%

Whites, 23%

Blacks, 8%

Whites, 4%

Blacks   Whites

■ Less than high school   ▨ High school   ■ Some college

FIG. 6.2. Percentage 30-34-Year-Old without BA, 2017
Source: Author's calculations based on U.S. Census Data, Educational
Attainment in the United States Table 1.

completing college. Black students are attending college, but a
smaller percentage reach that point, and those who enter college
graduate at lower rates than white students.

Explaining the Deficit

Many scholars have attempted to explain this deficit in the attainment of a college degree by black students. Reasons range from
inadequate academic preparation through insufficient finances to
unsupportive or hostile campus climates. Some research combines
two of these three factors in the same study but rarely all three.
Most research begins with the acknowledgment of the gap in college attendance between black and white students. Two factors
stand out in this research: academic preparedness and "socioeconomic" conditions or family background. The latter includes parents' education, family economic level, the number of siblings, and
the region of the country.

Of the socioeconomic factors, parents' education and economic
level stand out. According to one study, "Almost all blacks and
whites [children] from the highest socioeconomic background

stratum (read upper middle class and above) attend college."[5] Another study in the 1980s found that black children with college-educated parents were 85 percent more likely to enter college than children whose parents were high school dropouts.[6] Parental education level is a proxy for two distinct dynamics: a parent's ability to understand and shepherd a child through the complexity of college preparation and application (cultural capital), and the financial means to cover the ever-rising cost of a college education, even in state public school (economic capital). While there is a sizable black upper middle class (23 percent),[7] it is still smaller than the white upper middle class (33 percent). The lower middle class, the larger of the two strata of the black middle class, often lacks the financial resources to send their children to college. Black working-class families have even less financial resources to support college education for their children. The conclusion of two researchers is worth reproducing here:

> Many studies, including our own, clearly show that racial disparities in the *precollege* experience of black and white youth are responsible for blacks' overall lower rates of college attendance than whites' rates. That is, the persistent *total* gap favoring whites indicates blacks' continued disadvantage in exactly the factors that predict college attendance: Blacks are concentrated in the lowest socioeconomic strata and academic performance quintiles, are concentrated in public and Southern schools, and have more siblings than whites. That these resource characteristics favor whites produces the *total* black-white gap in college attendance. The main obstacles that block black youth from attending college exist *prior to submitting a college application.* Hence, the reduction and eventual elimination of the racial gap in *access* to higher education requires the improvement of the socioeconomic conditions and academic credentials of blacks.[8]

Although the authors note that black students are "concentrated in the lowest . . . academic performance quintiles," they do not analyze the reasons for this concentration. Given that a larger percentage of African American than white families live in less affluent areas and poor neighborhoods, their children often attend poorly funded schools. Black and other minority students are often tracked into non-college-preparatory classes and graduate from high school without the requisite courses for college. Many of those who defy the odds and attend college are handicapped from the beginning.

Getting into college is one thing; persisting to the end is another matter. The statistics on the percentage of adults with "some college" reveal that a high percentage of both black and white students who enter college fail to obtain degrees, presumably because of factors such as inadequate finances, lack of academic preparation, the "fit" of a particular institution, and campus climate. At least one study found that black students are as likely to graduate at predominantly white institutions as those who attend historically black colleges and universities (HBCUs),[9] while another study suggests that black students find a more supportive environment at HBCUs.[10] Clearly, the question of students' persistence to graduation requires more study. Not in dispute, however, is the close connection between education and occupational achievement.

This takes us back to the attainment model outlined earlier. Both the model and the statistics on educational attainment suggest that a bachelor's degree or higher leads to upper-middle-class careers; some college prepares students for the lower-middle-class technical, clerical, and sales occupations; and high school or below places students in manual or working-class jobs. The correlation is not perfect, but the connection between education and jobs is robust.

A Peak behind the Statistics: The Long Struggle to Reach the Top

The thirty-one couples I interviewed in Prince George's County, Maryland, offer a more in-depth understanding of the process of educational attainment that lies behind the statistics. These couples spoke about their individual experiences during the college application process, their choice of college, the majors they selected, the financing of their education, and their experiences on campus. All but six husbands and four wives had bachelor's degrees. Those without bachelor's had some college or were in school. Nine husbands and nine wives had also earned master's degrees, one husband and three wives were lawyers, and one wife had a doctorate.

THE COLLEGE ENTRANCE PROCESS

Anyone who has gone to college or has shepherded a child through the college application process understands how confusing and stressful this can be. There are the visits to college campuses, the application itself with the dreaded essay, FAFSA forms, and the wait for letters of acceptance, rejection, or wait-listing. For African American students, there is the added concern about campus climate, the percentage of minorities, and the school's openness to diversity. Should the final choice be a predominantly white college or a historically black college or university? How did these couples, as young students, negotiate the educational attainment process, and what choices did they make?

Given that the interviewees all shared the experience of choosing to live in black middle-class neighborhoods, it is tempting to assume that they would have also chosen HBCUs for their education. Their choices defied such a simple assumption. Less than half of the husbands (thirteen) and wives (fourteen) attended HBCUs. When I divided the group by age, I found that six couples had attended college during the 1970s, another fourteen graduated in the 1980s, and six in the 1990s. (The graduation dates of five could not be determined because of missing age data.) The oldest individual of the thirty-one couples was sixty-one, and the youngest was thirty-five. The couples, therefore, attended college against varying political and economic backgrounds, from the racial turmoil of the turbulent 1960s to the roaring economy of the 1990s. Below, I will analyze how the different political and economic climates influenced their college choices and experience.

The 1970s was the first full decade following the dismantling of segregation in higher education and public accommodations. As universities in southern and border states fell under federal mandates to desegregate both their student bodies and their faculties, African American students were now able, at least legally, to choose between HBCUs and the mostly white colleges and universities that had earlier rejected them. How did they choose? What was their experience in college?

Of the six couples (twelve individuals) who went to college and graduated during the 1970s, only one husband and two wives chose HBCUs. Their decision was not simply a choice between HBCUs and white colleges. Region of residence, finances, family educational background, knowledge of the process, and race all influenced their final decisions. The role of region was evident in several ways. Julia and Roy Bell, who grew up in Boston, both attended Northeastern University in that city and did not consider HBCUs. Dennis Gilbert, who lived in Des Moines, Iowa, attended nearby Drake University where his older brother was a student. When I asked whether he had thought about other schools, he responded, "No, I didn't. My father had died when I was seven. So it was kind of a case of Drake was close; and money-wise, that was probably what I could afford. My mother had to raise the three—my brother, myself, and my sister—by herself. So money-wise Drake was kind of the one."

Many colleges at this time recruited black students because of affirmative action requirements or altruism. Claudia Gilbert's choice of a white college in Holland, Michigan, fell in this category. Her explanation of how she went from St. Louis to Hope College in Michigan is also illustrative of the difficulties some of these recruited students encountered.

LANDRY: Did you think of some other schools? How did you end up in Holland, Michigan?

CLAUDIA: I believed the hype. I didn't really think of any other schools, and I don't know why I didn't. Because I didn't come from an environment where you wouldn't know. So, Hope came to my school and recruited. And they had this video, and it was lovely, and it was like fun. And it was this and that, and it was real. Going to school in St. Louis was a real challenge for me since leaving a rural area. And so when I moved to the big city there was so much going on in the school. It was just a lot for me, so I was trying to get away as an escape. So when they came, I said yeah. And they offered me money. So I said sure. But you know, it's really, really strange. I don't know why I didn't think of any other schools. And my parents never suggested that I do. I think they just wanted me to make that decision. 'Cause I have a sister. She went to Wichita State. Why didn't I think about Wichita State? I don't know. I thought my dad went there, but he didn't. My dad went to Stanford. So anyway, once I got there, the minute I drove on campus, I knew I had made a mistake.

LANDRY: How was that?

CLAUDIA: I could just tell. It had this other environment. You go into this town, and you see all this Dutch stuff. And I just knew I had made a mistake, . . . but I knew I didn't want to spend any more than four years in college. So I toughed it out.

The Harrisons and the Johnsons, who all went to the University of Maryland, illustrate the role of parents in the choice process. For the Harrisons, who entered college in the early 1970s, their mothers' influence proved decisive. As Joyce explained: "I kinda wanted to [go to an HBCU]. I lived in Baltimore, so I didn't want to go to Morgan [an HBCU in Baltimore]. I really wanted to go to Howard [an HBCU in Washington, D.C.]. My mother didn't want me to go to Howard. I got accepted at UCLA, Howard, and someplace else. My mother told me that I couldn't go anyplace that she couldn't drive to."

As he told it, Frank's experience was similar: "My mother wanted me to go to where she went to school, St. Paul's in Lawrenceville,

Virginia, or to Virginia Union where she went. She wanted me to be a teacher, 'cause she was a teacher. I didn't want to be a teacher. I said there's no money. But she wanted me to go to those places; but we decided on the University of Maryland. There were a lot of New Yorkers at the University of Maryland. A lot of the professors were from New Jersey or New York, so I said, 'Oh, I feel comfortable here.'"

The Johnsons, who grew up locally, also attended the University of Maryland and graduated in the late 1970s. Each came from very different educational backgrounds. While Alfred spoke proudly of being a third generation college graduate, and of his mother who earned a PhD in mathematics, Charlene recalled a different family experience. She noted, "We were not used to college at all in my family." Yet it was her father who, with just two years of college, filled out all the financial aid forms. Five of his six children attempted college, with two earning BAs. Charlene's mother only finished high school, and Alfred's father managed only two years of college.

Sometimes a sibling or other relative proved to be the decisive factor in choosing between an HBCU and a white college. Unlike Joyce Harrison, who wanted to go to Howard but could not because of her mother's opposition, Mary Douglas, a first-generation college student, followed in her brother's footsteps and attended Howard University. Explaining her choice, she said, "I had applied to Howard, American University, Lincoln, and maybe one of the schools in New Jersey, but I liked the Washington area, and I knew my brother had gone to Howard, so it was Howard for me." In doing so she became one of three siblings out of seven who earned college degrees.

Patrick Harrington and his wife, Judy, also went to HBCUs, although Patrick attended for only one semester. His experience reflects the influence of race in the Deep South during that period. As he explained, the segregated environment severely affected the aspirations as well as the opportunities of young African Americans.

In New Orleans in the early '70s, most [blacks] either went to the military, worked for the post office, or just got some old mediocre job. The only people that really went to college were those that were real smart, and they were gonna be the doctors or lawyers [and serve the black community]. As we saw it those were the only options that we had. Now we teach our kids that the options are endless; whatever piques your interest is what you should do. Back then we weren't told that. Here are your options: A, B, C, and D.

My uncle was trying to break that mold 'cause he had been to predominately white schools (the only black one in the family), the University of Wisconsin in the '60s. And that's where he got his doctorate. And so he was trying to change that mentality within the family, but he wasn't close enough to do that. He did enough to get me to Tuskegee [an HBCU in Alabama].

At another point in our conversation, Patrick mused about his choice of Tuskegee with a tinge of regret for only completing one semester there.

LANDRY: Well, do you know what made you decide on Tuskegee?
PATRICK: My uncle worked there. He was a professor at Tuskegee. And I had been there several times. My sister went there. It was gonna be a family thing. I had three sisters. My oldest sister went there. My next sister didn't go to college, and my last sister stayed in New Orleans and went to Xavier. That was why I selected it [Tuskegee]. And I needed to get away too. That was very important.

The experiences of Judy also show the obstacles sometimes faced by African American students who did not grow up in families with a history of college graduates, and the importance of adult mentorship. Although two siblings attended college without finishing, Judy did, finding the motivation, it seems, from her grandfather.

LANDRY: So how did you decide that you wanted to go to college?

JUDY: My grandfather.

LANDRY: He was a college kid? What did he do?

JUDY: He worked for these white people and spent a lot of time with their kids instead of working with his kids. And so he knew their abilities were no more than ours. And so he tried to instill in us that if they could do it you could do it. So he just made us promise, he made me promise that I would go to college. And so I did.

THE COLLEGE EXPERIENCE ON PREDOMINANTLY WHITE CAMPUSES IN THE 1970S

Two things influenced the experience of African American students on predominantly white campuses during the 1970s: academic support and race. The responses of several individuals revealed that academic support varied greatly from school to school. Some schools, with the assistance of federal and state funds, established support programs, such as Student Support Services (SSS) and Intensive Educational Development (IED), to assist first-generation black college students. Other schools did not. There could also be a disconnect between the existence of such programs and the reaction of white professors to black students' needs. Alfred Johnson recalled his struggle to keep up with the workload in the engineering department on one campus with a strong IED program. Rather than receiving help when he went to one of his white professors, the professor said, "It's in the book." He said, "It's in the book." Discouraged, he switched his major to advertising. To emphasize the grave consequences, Charlene added, "My husband would've been an engineer."

In his new major, he also encountered the common complaint of subjective grading. Alfred was cautious about claiming racism as he recalled his experience.

ALFRED: The school was a good experience. I do not take that from it. It taught me a lot, but again, it goes back to the race issue. I was in a curriculum that was subjective in grading. So it was a professor's opinion. Because design, it was opinion. It wasn't science; it wasn't right or wrong; it was an opinion. So if I got a B, did I really deserve the B, or did I just get the B because of who I was?

CHARLENE: They were *nigger-rating*; that's what we called it.

ALFRED: But was that a function of being in a predominately white institution where you can't really quantify whether your grade was justified, or was there some type of bias.

LANDRY: Was there a time when you felt that?

ALFRED: That grades had bias? Yes.

CHARLENE: Especially in the '70s.

Joyce Harrison viewed her undergraduate experience at the same university positively. "I had a good time," she said. But her graduate experience was remarkably different:

> I started in communications. I finished thirty credits at the University of Maryland in the Speech Communication department. And I'll never forget it. I had a woman that was my professor. She looked in my face one day—I had never gotten a C, and I had to have her for three more courses—and she told me black people could not write, and we were not good writers. And she said as long as she was there, I was not going to finish. And I didn't know anything about EEOC [Equal Employment Opportunity Commission]. So I picked up my marbles and I went to UDC [University of the District of Columbia], and I finished with honors in Instructional Systems Technology. I am a good writer. A very good writer. I do good research. But she said black people weren't good writers. And she told me that; it was just the two of us. And I had three more classes to take with her, and I knew it wasn't going to work.

Pursuing a college degree on a mostly white campus could be very challenging for black students during the 1970s. The lack of support from white professors, incidents of undeniable discrimination, and the small number of black students all made attendance at white colleges and universities challenging. Subjective grading, which at times left students uncertain whether white professors graded them fairly, was an added stress not experienced by white students. Of the scarcity of black students on campus, Joyce Harrison said, "There weren't any black people. You could hardly see any black people. You could walk all day and wouldn't see black people."

While Joyce reported no personal experiences of racism as an undergraduate, the remark of one white student underscored the kinds of racial prejudices and stereotypes some students brought from home to campus. "This one [white] girl said she was so amazed. Her mother had told her how black people were, and she said, 'You're not anything like my mother told me black people were. You wash every day, you're clean and everything.'"

COLLEGE SELECTION IN THE 1980S

The majority of the thirty-one couples attended college during the 1980s. When I interviewed them, most were in their forties (forty to forty-eight) except for two wives, one aged thirty-seven, the other fifty-one, who graduated in 1978. Out of fourteen couples, a slight majority—nine husbands and seven wives—had attended predominantly white colleges. Region, family, and finances were the most influential factors in explaining their choices.

My conversation with the Gardners, both of whom had attended white schools, revealed the complicated mixture of these factors.

LANDRY: So where did you go to school?

KAREN: Radford University.

LANDRY: What made you choose Radford?

KAREN: My guidance counselor went to Radford, and she said, "You know, I think it will be a good fit for you." And then the lady—I lived in a small town [in Virginia]—the lady at the bank went to Radford, and she said, "You know, I think you'd love it there." And then my best friend was going to Radford, too. So when I went to visit, it was a good fit. I wanted to go to USC

[University of Southern California]. I always thought, my whole life, I thought I would go to USC until my junior year and my dad was like, "Okay, let's just be realistic here. You ain't going to school in California." It was like, we can't afford it so that's why it [Radford] was a good fit, and they had a very, very good communications program.

LANDRY: Why did you choose Virginia Tech, Morris?

MORRIS: 'Cause I didn't get into the school I wanted to go to. I wanted to go to Princeton, and I didn't get in. I got accepted everywhere else but there. So I said, "Okay, I could go to these other schools." I wanted to get away; I wanted to leave D.C., I thought at that time. If I'm not mistaken it was cheaper for me, it was definitely cheaper for me to go there than to live on campus at Maryland. Plus if I went to Maryland, my parents probably would have wanted me to stay at home. So then a good friend of mine from high school had gone to school there, was in school there, was playing football. So I was like, I'm there.

Later the conversation turned to the subject of HBCUs.

LANDRY: Did either of you think about going to a predominantly black college?

KAREN: I will be honest. I considered no HBCU.

LANDRY: None?

MORRIS: To be honest, my parents were particular; [they] steered me away from that. My mom went to Federal City College. My dad didn't go to college. My dad, he is eighth grade. Okay. And they came from—this is just me, love them both—but where white people's ice was colder than black people's ice. So, you know, when I went to school, busing had started, and my mom was working up in Georgetown, so I went to school in Georgetown. And I went to Gonzaga [a private high school], so there wasn't even a question. I wasn't going to Howard. You know I wish to God I might have gone. But you know, I think no, not for me. Even if I had wanted, some way I would have been talked out of it.

KAREN: In my high school, no one [mentioned HBCUs]. I will be honest; I didn't know what an HBCU was until I probably was in college. One of my roommates failed out in the second semester . . . [went] to VA State [an HBCU], which is ten miles from where I grew up. I had never been there until I went to visit her. And there was a black girl at my high school who went to Hampton, I think. My guidance counselors never even mentioned Hampton, VA State, Spellman, none. They talked about UVA, about William and Mary, about Radford, about all these schools they thought would be a good fit for me, and none were predominantly black schools. And I don't think I would have gone to a predominantly black school because I think that would have been a culture shock for me.

MORRIS: For me, I had people in my high school who went to Xavier [an HBCU in New Orleans] and Howard, and it just wasn't something in my parents' mind, in their molding of me. I didn't think like that. I was going to Princeton, or I was going to Cornell. Like I said, I got in everywhere except for the place I wanted to go.

KAREN: But stereotypes too, because once I started to learn about HBCUs, people would say, "Oh, it's not as competitive, it's easy," that kind of thing. I think just stereotypes and lack of knowledge. I didn't know what an HBCU was; I had no idea.

While some parents did not know about HBCUs, it was rare to find any who opposed their child's attendance, as was the case with Morris Gardner's parents. This interview also showed that the choice of a white college sometimes resulted from both a lack of knowledge of HBCUs and a preference for a particular white college. The 1980s also brought a different calculus to the college choice by African American students. Attendance at a white college was less and less a novelty or a pioneering choice.

To some extent the choice process also differed by gender. Several of the African American men were offered and accepted athletic scholarships to white colleges. In Stephen Francis's case, race was also an important factor. He attended Salisbury University, a predominantly white school.

LANDRY: What made you choose Salisbury?
STEPHEN: My mother.
LANDRY: What?
STEPHEN: My mother.
MARGARET: And a scholarship.
STEPHEN: Yeah, yeah. I got some money for football. They gave me some incentives to come. I wanted to go in the military, but they [my parents] were like, "No, you're going to college." And just opposite of her [Margaret], I went to a predominately black high school. Bladensburg High School, which was predominately black, and still is. So they wanted me to have more of a white experience. Salisbury was about 95 percent white then; it's probably 99 percent white now. So they wanted me to have that experience. And it was, it was a good experience.

Although neither of Stephen's parents had gone to college, education was a priority for them. As Stephen noted, "They kind of stressed that they wanted that for us, I guess." A brother and two sisters with master's degrees attest to the success of their support.

John Berry also accepted an athletic scholarship to Duke University. That he went to Duke rather than a less prestigious university was due to an interesting coincidence.

I went to public school. I was gifted, and I played football. And when I got into the seventh grade in Pittsburgh's public school system, there was a gifted program for the eighth grade. Now of the twelve kids in the program, two of them were actually placed by taking a test, the other ten were by recommendations. One of my teachers did not recommend me, so I didn't get into the program. So eighth grade goes by. In ninth grade, I get called into the principal's office, Mr. Samuel. And he says, "Look at your grades here. How come you aren't in the gifted program?

Your grades are off the chart. I want you to take this test for the ABC program and to get a better chance and just see what happens." And so I took this test, I passed, and ended up going to this public boarding school in Philadelphia called Wagner. And you know, in my school, there were more National Merit Scholars than any public school in the nation. And I got a football scholarship to go to Duke, so I played football at Duke. But the whole course of my education changed in that moment when he [the principal] said, "You know what?" Someone took the time to go through my records. Now had I not gotten into that program, who knows where I'd be? I wouldn't have gone to Duke, certainly. My whole life would have taken a different turn. So luckily someone took enough time and interest in me.

Often, family finances were the decisive factor in school choice. Like Karen Gardner, who went to Radford instead of USC because of family finances, Betty Thomas's choice of a white in-state college was dictated by family finances. When I asked whether she had thought about going to an HBCU, she replied, "I didn't have the option. My father said, 'You're going to an in-state school 'cause that's what I can afford.' And that was it. For me, it would have been Michigan State or Ohio State 'cause my grandparents were there and they went to Michigan State. And that was it. It would have been nice [to go to an HBCU]."

Kay Berry's experience was similar.

LANDRY: Did you consider going to an HBCU?
KAY: For undergrad? No. I didn't have a lot of direction picking schools. My people didn't see very far outside Illinois. Like the biggest aspiration for me was to go to the University of Illinois, and I got in, but it was deemed too expensive, so I went to Southern Illinois, and then I started looking out. And I thought about Berkeley for grad school, because I had family out in California, which is kind of strange. But I kind of decided on my own to go to Howard [for graduate school]. And so, there's my HBCU right there.

THE COLLEGE EXPERIENCE ON PREDOMINANTLY WHITE CAMPUSES IN THE 1980S

By the mid-1980s, at least, African Americans on white campuses were less of a novelty than in the 1970s. Still, the number of black students remained small. As the following exchange with Karen and Morris Gardner revealed, how this affected a black student's campus life depended in part on his or her previous home experiences. As we saw earlier, Morris, who wanted to get away from home, chose a white college (Virginia Tech). Because of his home environment and education in black schools, Virginia Tech proved to be a challenging contrast.

MORRIS: Then when I went there it was funny that first weekend, that first month, month and a half; I went home every weekend because I hated it. Now, it's different. But at that particular time, the culture shock was just overwhelming, coming from D.C. and going to Blacksburg. It's totally different now, but when I lived there. Oh, my god. It was . . . but by the time it was time to graduate, I didn't want to leave.

LANDRY: Tell me about the culture shock.

MORRIS: I'll never forget this. The first day, my parents left me, they went home and I was in the dorm and the janitor was white. The janitor was white! I hate to put it that way but at that particular time, the only janitors I had seen in my schools were black. So the janitor in the dorm was white. Ma, they got a white janitor! So that started it all and then it was just different. There weren't any black radio stations at that time and the only way I could get one was coming out of Greensboro. And then there weren't that many of us in a school of 22,000 folks. There were only 1,000 of us down there. So I could go the whole day and might not see [another black student] other than back in the dorm. When I'm going to classes I could see two.

KAREN: At least you saw some. We could go days without seeing a black person.

MORRIS: You know, so, it was just, it was just too much. I was just not comfortable with the whole thing. But like I said after a while I got used to it and I got more active, went to more parties, and found out what was going on. And then you get used to it and as you're changing things are also changing. Time doesn't stand still for anybody. VA Tech had to adjust to those black people coming down there, as many as there were.

Karen, who came from a dissimilar background, reacted differently to the small number of black students on her campus.

KAREN: My experience was similar just in terms of the lack of diversity. When I was at Radford I guess we had about 6,000 students and only 200 African Americans, but my home experience was different. I was very accustomed to being the only black person in the class growing up. And like my best friend from high school who went to Radford was white. I think that Radford did a very good job in terms of really making sure that the campus was diverse and making sure that people felt comfortable and the same thing with VA Tech. We have a large portion of the students who came from Northern VA. If you were from Northern VA you were just a little bit more savvy, just in general. One of my roommates—because we were in a triple when I first went to Radford—was from a very small town, never had any experience with a black person ever. But it was a very positive experience for me, and I went home a lot that first semester, only because I was homesick. It was a great experience; and my best friends in life who are African American, we met at Radford, and two of them I talk to every day. But it was a great experience, great people, great professors.

MORRIS: There wasn't anything overt; it was just the cultural thing.

That seemed to be the story of many African American students' experiences on white campus in the 1980s, although Stephen Francis got into a physical fight when called the N-word. While he reported no other on-campus problems, he also noted that going off campus could be a challenge.

LANDRY: Was that kind of difficult sometimes?

STEPHEN: Sometimes, sometimes. I played football, so you know the football players got a little privileged at the school of course. But still you could tell once you got in the community that—

MARGARET: You weren't welcome.

STEPHEN: How whites looked at you. So that was different.

To ease the problem of small numbers and lack of support, many black students turned to black sororities, fraternities, and student unions for support and comfort. Charles Brody explained his experience at predominantly white Catholic University.

CHARLES: I also participated in the Black Student Union and ran it for about a year and a half.

LANDRY: I didn't know Catholic University had a black student union.

CHARLES: Oh yeah. There's a long history behind that, a long story behind that.

ROSE: He still keeps in touch with his friends.

CHARLES: It's crazy. We were kind of close-knit, and you had to be. I think I had an advantage, one 'cause I was local. But the second thing was because I automatically clicked in with that group, of which a significant amount participated in that same partnership scholarship program. I got the advantages of knowing what professors not to take, for instance. If they [black students] had taken exams, they would share the exam with you so you knew how that professor tested, that kind of stuff. So I got some inside knowledge and inside insight, on how to survive that first year in college.

The lack of this "inside knowledge," which white students often had, disadvantaged black students, as Joseph Howard, who had transferred from a white to a black college, recounted.

LANDRY: So how do you compare your experience before UDC [University of the District of Columbia, an HBCU]?

JOSEPH: Man, it's like night and day, with respect to when you have a professor tell you that this is not the major for you. Or you don't have the support mechanism to get through the classes like other people had, and I went through my first year [in Iowa State University] without those support mechanisms.

LANDRY: Because you're black.

JOSEPH: Well, I think so because when I finally figured it out, it was the white kids who showed me what I needed to do. Because they knew it. I'm in my second year behind the curve, so they know what to do. And they got it on the first day as freshmen.

LANDRY: When you say "support system," what do you mean?

JOSEPH: Well, I didn't know until the first semester sophomore [year] that the white fraternities had a test bank of all the tests for all the classes dating back twenty years. So if you had a physics professor that had been there fifteen years and he taught physics in a class of five hundred, you can pull his test and study the test. I didn't learn that until the second year. So I was getting crushed my first year. And you got a professor telling you that this isn't the major for you and you really should do something else. So you know, kind of just getting beat down and then going into classes with five hundred people and you're the only African American. So of course when you raise your hand or if you don't know what you're doing or if you don't know an answer, you're picked out of the crowd. And then not having enough African Americans ahead of me to be able to tell me the secrets. But then I finally figured it out, and some of the white students who I became friends with helped me figure it out. But by that time my grades were in a tank, and I was trying to recover. And it was very difficult. So I ended up changing my major; and you know I probably would not have changed if I were at an HBCU. I probably would have stayed in the major I had originally intended. And I had just gotten brainwashed by my parents, you know, by my parents. 'Cause I had a full scholarship to Morehouse and didn't go.

Those who chose an HBCU over a white college or university did so for one of two reasons: family experience with HBCUs or reaction to their high school racial experience. Brenda White, who had grown up in Chicago, spoke forcefully of her decision to select an HBCU: "I really wanted to go to a black college because I had grown up in predominantly white neighborhoods, and I went to predominantly white schools, and I felt I wanted to get into an environment where I could really connect. And so that's kind of why I looked for black universities." Similarly, Margaret Francis, who had attended an all-girls mostly white prep school, wanted something different. Her answer to my question about school choice was straightforward: "I had had enough of that. I just knew I wanted to go to an HBCU. And Howard was first on my list. There were only four black girls in my graduating class. I had traveled a little bit. I just wanted to be around some progressive black folk. That's how I felt."

Several respondents noted that their family members' history with HBCUs motivated them to follow in their footsteps. Brian Thomas, who chose an HBCU, talked about the many family members who attended this school over several generations.

BRIAN: Well, my grandmother went to my college, and three of her daughters went there, and I got a scholarship. And I knew I always wanted to go to an HBCU and not a white university.

LANDRY: Because?

BRIAN: That's what I grew up being exposed to. The bands, the fraternities, the homecomings. And they do it a little different than white students. You know, it's more of a family setting. You know, you go to homecoming and you may see four or five of your friends or classmates. At black colleges, you go back and you see people that you hadn't seen in fifteen years, but then we come back and it's more of a family, it's more of a network of friends and family.

LANDRY: And that's what you found?

BRIAN: That's what I grew up around. My uncle worked at the university. He was dean of computer science at the time. Back then he was in charge of the data processing, etc. So that's where my experience stems from.

LANDRY: You're kind of a university brat, huh?

BRIAN: You know. My grandmother's sisters, she had three sisters who graduated from there. And three kids. It's kind of a no-brainer.

Debbie Hamilton also used the word "family" in describing her HBCU experience. "I loved it. I loved it, and we still go back now every year. It's like a family thing to go back to A&T [North Carolina A&T State University]. We are still close with our friends at A&T. We have homecoming every year, and our children are all ready to go."

Both Christine and Steve Edwards chose HBCUs when they were ready to attend college. Christine followed her brother, who had studied in the same university, while both of Steve's parents and his brother and sister graduated from HBCUs. He summed up his feelings about HBCUs versus white schools, saying, "I applied to one white school and that was the University of Delaware only because they were offering me a scholarship, but it was never really something that I would consider, 'cause I didn't want to go to a white school. I never even thought about it. I didn't consider it." Like Brenda White and Margaret Francis, Christine was also motivated by the desire for a black experience in college. "See," she noted, "I grew up in Florida, and I went to school with white kids. I was ready for an HBCU."

THE COLLEGE EXPERIENCE IN THE 1990S

By the 1990s, the number of African American students on white campuses had increased significantly. While Joyce and Frank Harrison had complained that they could go all day without seeing another black student on campus, Susan Snow, who graduated from a white university in 1992, offered as one reason for her satisfaction that there were "a lot of black people on campus, so I was happy with that." This was the same school about which Joyce Harrison, who graduated in the mid-1970s, complained, "You could walk all day and wouldn't see black people." Still, most of those in my sample who graduated in the 1990s had attended an HBCU. Robert Williams, who had attended both, two years at an HBCU and the rest of his college years at a white school, gave a vivid contrast of his experiences. He first described the impact of his two years at the HBCU.

> I pretty much grew up. I learned who I was in my first semester, first year. So I was fortunate to the extent that I was afforded the opportunity to go somewhere. And I did really well in high school. Like I said, I learned about life really when I got to college. Where I grew up black people only did one thing, or not one thing, a couple of things. I mean they played, for example, sports, basketball, football. And where I grew up, you know, it wasn't a progressive area. It was not a progressive area for black folks overall, so you had a limited view of what people do. And I get to Hampton and black people are playing tennis, on the swim team, chess club. I mean you see things that you didn't have exposure to, so you know it was a great experience from that perspective, 'cause it gave me kind of a better view of what people are about. And people are not, black people are not all the same. They like different things. And when you start looking at the bigger picture of the world, you see—like to give you an example—soccer is something I played when I was growing up. I was the only black on the soccer team in high school. But you know, you can go to another country and you'll see. Go to Nigeria. That's their sport. You know, that's just an example. So you just have a better understanding. A lot of that just comes from being exposed to other things besides what you, what you really think is out there.

Transferring to Old Dominion in his junior year placed Robert in a very different world.

I've been in both environments. Old Dominion is the opposite. What I saw there was—I mean, it's a bigger school and especially in engineering, and I'm sure it was in other disciplines—white folks stuck together, and the few black folks that were in my classes we stuck together. So that's all we ever had. That's all we had. We had each other. They had all the old tests they would never give us. You may befriend one or two, and there may be some harmonization there, but for the most part, you gotta rely on other folks. So we had an organization, and Hampton had it too, the National Society of Black Engineers. But at Old Dominion, that was really important for us to stick together to help each other. At Hampton it's there because it's an all-black school. But at Old Dominion, you needed it as a crutch to kind of inspire everybody else to try to get through 'cause it was tough. And nobody was looking out for you. And you had to get in there, you had to really just do your best to get through it. But the organization allowed us to help. People were in different disciplines, but we came together at the meetings, we could inspire folks, we had conferences that we went to, and we just had a good support system there. So that was really important, especially if you go to a place that they don't have your interests, that you have some type of organization that could help you through it.

Despite the difficulties, Robert persevered at the white university. The 1990s had brought some significant changes for black college students. He was not told to change his major, as had been the case with Joseph Howard during the 1980s. Unlike Joseph, having other black students for support, he endured and earned a degree in his chosen field.

While a large percentage of African American students still choose predominantly white colleges and universities, those who attend HBCUs often extol their merits over white schools for both the academic support they received and the comfort of their social life. Speaking of her time at an HBCU, Laura Williams spoke enthusiastically of an epiphany: "We both went to historically black colleges, and that's where, I always tell people, that's where I grew up. Because that's when the lights came on, and oh my God, I am somebody, you know? So, we want that for our kids." Explaining her choice of an HBCU over a white school, she said, "You know, I had also applied to Rutgers. I didn't apply anywhere that I didn't get in, but there was no desire there. Like, I couldn't look at the [white] campus and say, 'Oh, wow. I want to go here.' I felt like I could go to a historically black college and get all the tools that I need, and I think that was the best choice. I'm so glad I did."

African Americans have struggled to acquire the ticket to the middle class: a college education. The end of segregation in southern colleges and universities enlarged the pool beyond HBCUs, resulting in an increase in the number of black students who earn bachelor's degrees and higher. College choices depend on a variety of factors, including cost, location, family history, and personal preferences. Yet a large gap between black and white college attainment persists into the twenty-first century. In the following chapter, I turn to the final step in the attainment process: entry into the labor force.

7
From School to Work

A college degree is the second stage, but only the second stage, in the attainment process. Saying that does not diminish the significance of education but signals that the attainment process is not yet complete. From the point of view of Weber, a college degree is a "coin" to be traded in the market for one of the many positions of the middle class. This is true regardless of race, ethnicity, or gender. Yet the graduate's race, ethnicity, or gender has historically influenced this transition in a positive or negative manner. The negative impact of race was reflected in the remarks of Patrick Harrington, whom I quoted in the last chapter complaining of the limited range of occupations open to black college graduates during the 1970s. In chapter 2 of my 1987 book, *The New Black Middle Class*, I discussed improvements in the occupational attainment of members of the new black middle class compared to those in the old black middle class. While the old black middle class was restricted to professional occupations serving the black community, the new black middle class that emerged after the Civil Rights Act of 1964 entered a greater variety of occupations, including many in mainstream areas of the economy. It remains to be seen whether this trend continued during the decades following the civil rights era. The increase in black students' college and graduate school attainment, documented in chapter 6, suggests that much has also changed in the occupational attainment of blacks over the past decades. Whether this change has brought occupational parity with whites in the twenty-first century is the question I will now turn to using both discrete occupational rankings and a summary measure of inequality, the index of dissimilarity (ID).

The index of dissimilarity is a measure of the change that must occur to equalize two distributions. Its variation from 0 to 100 makes it an intuitive and useful measure in social science research. Any number over 0 indicates the percentage of individuals who would have to *change place* to equalize two distributions. In a comparison of the occupational distributions of blacks and whites, any number *greater* than 0 represents the percentage of black workers who would need to upgrade occupations to equalize their occupational distributions with that of white workers. An index of 0 would designate parity in their occupational distributions.[1] I use the IPUMS-USA data in this comparison for the years 1970, 1980, 1990, and 2000.[2] For these comparisons, I focus only on those middle-class occupations classified as "professional" by the Census Bureau. These, along with administrative/executive occupations, are "upper-middle-class" occupations and are therefore a test of black achievement at the highest level of the occupational structure. What does a comparison of the dissimilarity index tell us about black upper-middle-class achievement since 1970?

In 1970, the ID for the occupational distributions of all black and white professionals (males and females) was 0.256, showing that almost 26 percent of blacks would have had to change occupations (upgrade) to produce equal racial distributions. (It was 0.225 in 1980, 0.219 in 1990, and 0.200 in 2000.) Since in 1970 the occupational attainment of blacks had been severely blocked by segregation and discrimination, the index measures the degree to which blacks were denied access to the professional stratum of the upper middle class in 1970. There are also interesting gender differences. The index of dissimilarity for black and white male professionals was far larger (0.364) than for black and white professional females (0.149). Black male professionals needed a 36 percent *upgrading* in 1970 compared to only a 15 percent *upgrading* of black female professionals. In part, this reflects the limited professional occupations open to women, black or white, in 1970. Both experienced disadvantages in comparison to white males. Between 1970 and 2000, the equalization process improved somewhat to 0.200 or by a little over 5 percent (.056), with most of the upgrading occurring between 1970 and 1980, leaving black professionals still 20 percent behind whites in 2000. The 1980s and '90s witnessed an actual deceleration in the rate of black professional attainment. As in 1970, the racial dissimilarity index remained higher among black and white males (0.259) than among black and white females (0.164).

Occupational Concentration and the Top Ten

To better understand racial differences in occupational attainment, I compare discrete census occupations, standardized by IPUMS-USA for the decades 1980, 1990, and 2000. Ranking occupational titles by race and gender offers a more detailed measure of differences in the occupational attainment of black and white college graduates. I focus on occupations that the Census Bureau classifies as "professional," a group in the upper middle class that is more easily identified and understood. Some caveats should be remembered in interpreting these data. Not all occupations classified as professional by the Census Bureau are included in the IPUMS data sets. The number of these occupations vary from decade to decade as new ones are added and others removed. Hence, creating comparability across decades required some collapsing and some recoding of titles. Further, although labeled "professional" to distinguish these occupations from lower-middle-class and working-class occupations such as X-ray technician, salesperson, or carpenter, professional occupations include considerable variation in compensation, rank, and mobility opportunities. Even among occupations with the same title, there are significant variations. Teachers and engineers are good examples of this. A teacher may work at the primary or secondary level, may work in a public or private school, and may be a novice or senior professional. An engineer may be mechanical, chemical, or civil. Doctors have different specialties, and lawyers may work solo or in small or large firms, all of which affect compensation and benefits. Comparisons across race and gender both highlight and obscure these differences, depending on the degree to which titles are combined or separated. In general, these comparisons will underestimate the extent of racial and gender inequality.

To manage comparisons across so many occupational titles, I limit myself to the top ten *most common* in each racial and/or gender group. In 1980, elementary school teachers topped the list as the most common professional occupation among blacks and whites, both males and females. Behind this similarity, groups differed considerably in their racial and gender representations. Elementary school teachers were a far higher percentage of female professionals (29.4 percent of whites and 34.4 percent of blacks) than of male professionals (8.8 percent of whites and 14 percent of blacks). (See Tables 7.1 and 7.2.) The primacy of the elementary

TABLE 7.1. Percentage of Black and White Female Professionals, 1980

NO.	PROFESSIONS OF BLACK FEMALES	% OF PROFESSION	NO.	PROFESSIONS OF WHITE FEMALES	% OF PROFESSION
1	Teachers, elementary	34.4	1	Teachers, elementary	29.4
2	Registered nurses	16.0	2	Registered nurses	20.4
3	Social workers	10.9	3	Teachers, secondary	8.2
4	Teachers, secondary	7.5	4	Social workers	4.2
5	Teachers, kindergarten	4.6	5	Teachers*	3.6
6	Counselors	2.8	6	Designers	3.1
7	Teachers*	2.4	7	Teachers, kindergarten	3.0
8	Librarians	2.3	8	Librarians	2.6
9	Dietitians	2.3	9	Teachers, postsecondary	2.4
10	Teachers, postsecondary	1.7	10	Editors and reporters	1.8
		84.9			78.9

SOURCE: Author's calculations from U.S. Census 1980.
*Not elsewhere classified.

TABLE 7.2. Percentage of Black and White Male Professionals, 1980

NO.	PROFESSIONS OF BLACK MALES	% OF PROFESSION	NO.	PROFESSIONS OF WHITE MALES	% OF PROFESSION
1	Teachers, elementary	14.0	1	Teachers, elementary	8.8
2	Social workers	8.9	2	Lawyers	7.2
3	Teachers, secondary	6.4	3	Teachers, secondary	5.8
4	Clergy	5.5	4	Physicians	5.5
5	Teachers, postsecondary	4.4	5	Electrical engineers	4.9
6	Counselors	3.4	6	Teachers, postsecondary	4.7
7	Teachers*	3.3	7	Clergy	4.5
8	Physicians	3.2	8	Engineers*	3.8
9	Electrical engineers	2.9	9	Mechanical engineers	3.3
10	Lawyers	2.8	10	Civil engineers	3.2
		54.8			51.7

SOURCE: Author's calculations from U.S. Census 1980.
*Not elsewhere classified.

school teacher profession continued into the 1990s with only a slight decrease in their concentration among black (32 percent) and white (28 percent) female professionals. Not until 2000 was the first-place position of the elementary school teacher challenged by other professional occupations. (Since I am analyzing decennial censuses, the change may have occurred sooner than 2000.)

As a sign of the increasing importance of computers in the economy of 2000, computer systems analysts and computer scientists combined seized first place in the professional occupation rankings among both black and white males, with 13.9 and 10.9 percent of all professionals in their respective groups. (See Table 7.3.) In 1980, these digital professions ranked thirteenth and twelfth, respectively, among white and black males. Gains in the new economy came slower for women, despite the tremendous need that the dot-com bubble had generated for digital skills. By 2000, computer systems analysts and computer scientists ranked only fifth and eighth in frequency among black and white female

TABLE 7.3. Percentage of Black and White Male Professionals,
2000–2002

NO.	PROFESSIONS OF BLACK MALES	% OF PROFESSION	NO.	PROFESSIONS OF WHITE MALES	% OF PROFESSION
1	Computer systems analysts	13.9	1	Computer systems analysts	10.9
2	Social workers	8.8	2	Lawyers	7.6
3	Teachers, elementary	6.0	3	Teachers, secondary	6.5
4	Teachers, secondary	5.7	4	Electrical engineers	6.0
5	Electrical engineers	5.4	5	Physicians	5.4
6	Teachers*	5.3	6	Teachers*	3.8
7	Clergy	5.3	7	Teachers, elementary	3.8
8	Lawyers	3.1	8	Mechanical engineers	3.5
9	Physicians	2.4	9	Clergy	3.3
10	Designers	2.3	10	Designers	3.1
		58.2			53.9

SOURCE: Author's calculations from CPS data 2000 and 2002, combined to produce a larger sample.
*Not elsewhere classified.

professionals. (See Table 7.4.) Other race and gender group differences stood out in 2000. Black females were the only group with elementary school teachers still in first place. Among white females, elementary school teachers slipped down to second place, replaced by registered nurses.

Women, both black and white, were notably disadvantaged relative to males in 2000 by their greater concentration in the public sector, where compensations are lower. Of the top ten professional occupations in terms of frequency among women, only four among whites (nurses, first; designers, seventh; computer workers, eighth; and lawyers, tenth) were in the private sector. (See Table 7.4.) Black females fared slightly worse, having only three private-sector occupations in the top ten: nurses, (second), computer workers (fifth), and lawyers (tenth). Although professional males also worked in the public sector as teachers and social

TABLE 7.4. Percentage of Black and White Female Professionals,
2000–2002

NO.	PROFESSIONS OF BLACK FEMALES	% OF PROFESSION	NO.	PROFESSIONS OF WHITE FEMALES	% OF PROFESSION
1	Teachers, elementary	17.3	1	Registered nurses	17.6
2	Registered nurses	16.7	2	Teachers, elementary	16.9
3	Social workers	11.4	3	Teachers, secondary	7.3
4	Teachers, kindergarten	7.2	4	Teachers*	5.2
5	Computer system analysts	5.2	5	Teachers, kindergarten	4.8
6	Teachers*	4.8	6	Social workers	4.2
7	Teachers, secondary	4.6	7	Designers	3.7
8	Counselors	2.9	8	Computer system analysts	3.5
9	Teachers, special ed.	2.7	9	Teachers, special ed.	3.1
10	Lawyers	2.2	10	Lawyers	2.1
		75			68.4

SOURCE: Author's calculations from CPS data 2000 and 2002, combined to produce a larger sample.
*Not elsewhere classified.

workers, those in the top ten professions were far more likely to be in the private sector. (See Table 7.3.) Private-sector professions included four of the top five among white males (computer workers, first; lawyers, second; electrical engineers, fourth; and physicians, fifth) and two in the next five (mechanical engineers, eighth; designers, tenth). Although computer professionals ranked first among black males, the only other private-sector profession in their top five was electrical engineer, ranked fifth. The remaining three private-sector professions were in the next five: lawyers, eighth; physicians, ninth; and designers, tenth. Clergymen also held a higher rank among black males (seventh) than white males (ninth).

The good news in this story is the increasing diversity among black professionals that has accompanied greater access to higher education. Similar to black educational attainment, however, the occupational attainment of blacks at the highest levels (professionals) remains behind that of whites. It is tempting to point to the highest occupational achievements of blacks as examples of progress—a Supreme Court justice, astronauts, and CEOs of Fortune 500 companies—forgetting that in these exceptional occupations, blacks still fall far short of white attainment. Blacks account for only 1.2 percent of Fortune 500 CEOs, although blacks are 13 percent of the U.S. population. By even the rosiest assessment of black occupational attainment, the data show that the pace is far too slow. A large volume of social science research also reveals that black professionals are further handicapped in career mobility, access to supervisory positions, and income attainment.[3] While census data are unequaled in presenting the "big picture" of occupational attainment, they lack the details underlying the big picture. To fill in the gaps, I turn to my interviews with upper-middle-class couples in the Prince George's County suburbs.

The Transition from College to Work

The thirty-one families (sixty-two individuals) I interviewed entered the labor market between 1974 and 1994, a period that covered the early years following the Civil Rights Act of 1964 through the deep recession of the early 1980s to the boom years of the 1990s. During this time, the economy moved from typewriters and paper-and-pencil record keeping to a digital economy. When and how did these sixty-two women and men make their first entry into the labor force to claim their own class position? How did they find their first job? Was it the work for which they had trained? Was their progress made easier by strategic mentors along the way? Were unexpected obstacles the norm?

1968–1982

Six couples (twelve individuals) graduated and entered the labor force during the earliest decades following the Civil Rights Act of 1964. They were among the first to benefit from desegregation in higher education and the support of affirmative action in the labor market. During the late 1970s, programs designed to implement the mandate of the Great Society initiative also ended.

Joyce and Frank Harrison are typical of many black college graduates who entered the labor force during this period and found their first jobs in a federal government–funded program. Frank, who graduated from the University of Maryland in 1979 with a bachelor's degree in experimental psychology, landed his first job as an institutional counselor at a maximum-security prison for juvenile delinquents. As he explained, it was an easy transition from college to work. "I had graduated from the University of Maryland at College Park in 1979, and the first job I had was at Oakhill Youth Center. I went to 1900 U Street OPM, [Office of Personnel Management] and I filled out one of those little job applications, the 171S, 171. And they said, 'Oh, we have a job for you in Laurel, Maryland. It's the Department of Health and Human Services D.C. Oak Hill Youth Center, maximum juvenile prison.'" The transition from school to work, after graduating in 1974, was similarly smooth for Joyce. With her communications major, she found a position as a speech instructor in a program at a nearby university while she was working on a master's degree in instructional systems technology at UDC [University of the District of Columbia].

Despite the initial easy transition into the world of work, both soon discovered that there were limitations. After three years, Joyce received a pink slip with the terse message: "As of August we no longer need your services due to budget cuts." Frank was laid off after one year and, like Joyce, ended up at Jobs Corps, a program of President Johnson's Great Society initiative. For Frank, the transition was facilitated by a counselor at his previous job who encouraged him to apply for a position as a guidance counselor at the nearby Jobs Corps. Joyce recalled her own movement to Jobs Corps partly in religious terms: "I can't say anything more than I've been blessed, to be at the right place at the right time. It wasn't nothing but God because the day that my unemployment ran out I got a call from Job Corps. It's like you put good stuff out in the universe. Thank God you get it back."

Sociologists think of careers as vertical moves in the same occupation ("climbing a ladder") or as horizontal moves in the same occupational area or using the same skills and training. The latter describes the professional careers of Edith and Michael Jamison. When I interviewed them in 2007, Michael described his position as the "drug czar" at Homeland Security. It was his sixth job over a period of almost two decades, during which he moved through many federal government departments. Edith held a position as a mediator at the Department of Labor, utilizing the skills she had honed over the years. For her, at least, it was the fulfillment of her desire to work in the more secure environment of the federal government than in the private sector. Edith explained, "You see, government was secure. Because I had a lot of friends who worked in private industry, and then the next thing you know they would let them go. And I couldn't understand how you were working somewhere and making a good sum and then somebody will tell you, 'Well, next week I want you to get all your things.' And then you have to look for a job." "'You are terminated. I don't like the way you dress,'" added her husband. Edith continued, "You know they could terminate you in private industry; they don't have to have just cause. You know you just want a good fit, so I knew that there was some stability. I'm not a real big risk taker in some aspects of my life. And job security—that's the one thing I knew about the federal government."

A career in the safer environment of the federal government was a common path for many black college graduates in this period, but not for all. Claudia and Dennis Gilbert represent divergent paths. Upon graduation in 1973 from Hope College in Holland, Michigan, with double majors in English and communications, Claudia took a job as a reporter in nearby Grand Rapids. A year later, she furthered her studies at Columbia University in New York City, where she was hired by United Press International and sent on assignment to their office in Des Moines, Iowa. For almost three decades, she pursued a typical journalism career that included stints at *USA Today* and the Associated Press. When we met, Claudia had recently completed a graduate program in journalism and was a professor at American University. She described the change as the result of "a midlife crisis." Demonstrating the complexity and difficulty of career changes, she struggled to explain her motivation. "I figured that I needed to do something different, and this was . . . either now or never. And I had the opportunity with the fellowship [to pursue graduate work]. So, that's why I went back [to school]." When I commented that this was a big change, she responded, "It's a big change. But I think it's kind of fun 'cause it's something different. And I was getting to the point where I felt old as a reporter. And I know there's a lot of old reporters; but see, I was covering education. And for most news organizations, that's the beat that the young folk come through. And so, I didn't want to go to the press conferences and know that [I'm] the oldest one in the bunch and that sort of stuff. But I just thought it's time for a change." Claudia's work as a journalist for almost thirty years closely resembles the vertical career pattern, even with four moves through several organizations. The switch to academia as a professor of journalism placed her in a different area of the same field.

Dennis graduated in 1971 after a three-year interruption that took him to Vietnam as a draftee. Upon his return, he completed his last year of college at Drake University with a degree in accounting. The Internal Revenue Service recruited him on campus, and he worked as an auditor until 1987, first in Des Moines and then in Washington, D.C. Except for the stint in Vietnam, Dennis's transition from college to work was as smooth as it can get. Being recruited on campus relieved him of the drudgery of sending out dozens of résumés and traveling for interviews. His position with the IRS ended after his move to Washington, D.C., with a pink slip. He described that point in his career in philosophical terms: "When I left IRS, I guess they were trying to tell me I wasn't working, or I was in the office too much. So they gave me a pink slip, and so I then got into the hands-on computer programming.

And so, in effect, I left before the pink slip time came up, but they had given me a pink slip."

From there, he transitioned to a computer programming position with the army as a civilian, a job he still held at the time of my interview. Having only two different jobs on his résumé, Dennis had one of the least complicated career histories. It was otherwise for Roy Bell. His career spanned seven jobs after graduating in 1976 with a major in criminal justice from Northeastern University in Boston. Apart from the many positions he held over thirty years, Roy's history is also an example of the dilemma some black college graduates faced at this time. Beginning with a personal philosophy of remaining on a job for only two years, "learn one year, give back a year, move on, increase my salary," Roy moved rapidly through his first two jobs first with Boston Hospital in Human Resources then with Miter as a salesman. His third job with the Bank of Boston brought an unexpected challenge. As Sharon Collins documents in her book *Black Corporate Executives*, in the aftermath of the Civil Rights Act, many corporations responded to the pressure to hire more African Americans by creating special positions focused on the black community. It was such a position that the Bank of Boston had in mind when it hired him to work in Human Resources. His disappointment led to his departure after just one month. As he explained, "They promised me that I would be involved with hiring for specialty-type positions, and when I got there the specialty-type positions were recruiting for minorities. That wasn't what I wanted. I wanted more mainstream type work; so I left there. And I had a choice at that time, of going with either Bank of Boston or Boston Medical. So I went with Bank of Boston 'cause I came in as an officer. So I found what was really going on and you know. I told them I didn't come here to do that. I was really looking to do more work mainstream. And then they wanted to try to keep me on, make some more promises. And I just didn't see anything happening, so I left."

After a four-week hiatus, Roy was back at Boston Medical in Human Resources, where he remained for six and a half years until he and his wife moved to Maryland in 1989. A brief stint of self-employment as a headhunter did not work out, and the tight labor market of the early 1990s found him returning to Boston Medical and a long commute until he found a local job with Visa a year and a half later.

Like her husband, Julia Bell earned a college degree from Northeastern University in Boston. Although she majored in education, she felt that her extensive co-op experience as a student in the health-care field led to her first job at Boston City Hospital as a manager of two ambulatory care clinics in the outpatient facility. After two years, she moved to an insurance company. She noted, "It was my management experience that got me into the insurance company. And I stayed there for nine years." The family's move to Prince George's County in Maryland led to yet another job, this one as a manager in the registrar's office of Prince George's Community College, where she stayed for ten years. Afterward, she accepted a position at Howard Hospital. Altogether, during the years following graduation, Julia held four different jobs, all in some management capacity in health care or education. Her careers fall into the horizontal pattern.

On Being a First. The 1970s and early '80s was a period of transition for black college graduates entering the labor market. Even when there was no overt racism on the job, there were occasions of discomfort or pressures not encountered by whites. This was the case with Brenda White, who experienced career success after graduating with a degree in accounting from Howard University but also encountered race-related pressures.

LANDRY: What was your first job after graduating?
BRENDA: Oh, my first years. I started out as an accountant, and I guess I went up to financial manager.
LANDRY: In the same job?
BRENDA: No, different companies. And I guess that's another thing. In a lot of my companies, I was always the first black. And so that added pressure. At the *Atlanta-Journal Constitution*, I was

the first black financial manager for the newspaper. So, I'd even get blacks coming in [saying], "Don't mess it up because they'll never hire another one of us." So, little comments. At *USA Today*, I was the first black budgeting supervisor, budgeting manager for the newspaper. So the same thing: "Don't mess it up because you know . . ." Now they [white employees] can mess up, and they'll still hire more whites. But I can't mess up because I'm carrying the whole race.

For other black college graduates, there was often the "loneliness" of being in companies with few blacks. Speaking of this period Brenda's husband, Andrew, who worked for Westinghouse as a mechanical designer, commented, "There were probably four blacks in the whole building." With Karen Gardner, it was the annoyance of ignorance or stereotypes held by otherwise well-meaning white colleagues or managers.

LANDRY: How did you get your first job?

KAREN: After sending out sixty-five résumé tapes I got one call back, from Peoria, Illinois, saying we got a job for you. And Morris and I had just got married.

MORRIS: About a year.

KAREN: Well, just got married, and Mark was like, "I'm not moving to Peoria." And I understood because he would have had to take such a big salary cut, and plus we knew I wasn't gonna be there for a long time; so we had a commuter marriage for about a year and a half. I'll never forget: sixty-five résumé tapes, and I got one call back.

LANDRY: What was your experience like?

KAREN: It was a good experience, only because I knew it was a means to an end. It was different because I am definitely not a Midwest kind of gal, and people in the Midwest have certain perceptions about people from the East Coast. They think we are all city slickers, and like I said I worked with a cameraman. We were both like the low people on the totem pole. He was the newly hired cameraman; I was the newly hired reporter. He had no experience with black people and just had all of these stereotypes. And I remember one day he asked me, "So let me ask you something because I don't want to offend you because I offended Elizabeth" who was a Jewish woman who worked there. He said, "So I don't want to offend you, but do black people celebrate Christmas?" You mean the birth of Christ? I'm like, yes. "Okay, well I just wanted to ask because I didn't know that Jews didn't celebrate Christmas; I offended her." So you know that was what my experience was like. But there were African Americans there, and fortunately for me, I am in a sorority. So a lot of times when you move . . . what you do is just look up your chapter that's there. Usually, there's a chapter or there are some sorors or somebody who can kind of help you, you know get integrated, well not integrated but just involved in the community. But you know, I'm glad I had the experience. Looking back in retrospect, I'm glad I went there. I'm glad I did it, but it was just constantly that way—stereotypes all the time. I remember my assignment editor liked every story idea I had. A lot of times, my stories were like let's get the African American perspective on this, you know, that kind of thing. And one day he says to me: "You know, I just don't want anybody to think that it's me, that I'm giving you all these stories to go out and get the African American perspective, and so, you know, why don't you think of some more things." I said, "Wow, that's interesting because Anna and Frasier and Scott and Joe and Derek and Susan, they do stories about white people every day." He's like, "Oh, I never thought about it like that. Well, keep 'em coming, keep 'em coming." But it was a good experience, and I hope that my experience there, I hope that some people learned some things from me too. But it was exciting times, because black people were like, "Oh my gosh, we're so glad we saw you on the air, and gosh we were so glad it's a black person." So that was always very nice too.

Time. Finding a dream job after graduating from college often requires time. Several respondents reported setting their sights on a particular job and demonstrated admirable persistence until it was achieved. Kay Berry, who was a *Washington Post* reporter, talked about the difficulty she had pursuing this job. "I was a little more spotty [than her husband, John]," she admitted. After graduating with a degree in journalism, she enrolled in a master's program in sociology at Howard University because, she said, "I wanted a perspective to write out of. So I thought sociology would give me that."

This decision led to a long detour, but she persisted. "I had a job in '89/'90, a full-time job in a think tank, you know as a secretary (while studying for the master's degree). Then I got a promotion, so I had to really make a decision. Am I gonna try to get into journalism? And if I am, I have to do it now, entry level, because I won't be able to once I start making money. I won't be able to quit the job I was at, at this think tank, where they liked me and they were grooming me." She then made a tough decision, only to encounter a serious roadblock. "I quit that and I tried to get a job in journalism. Well, there was a contraction in journalism, plus I didn't have any experience . . . never worked for a daily paper as an intern or anything, never even worked for my school paper. My people were teachers. They didn't know about internships. All I knew is you go to college, you get a degree, you get a job. And so I didn't have any clips or anything. Started temping, couldn't get a job in journalism, not at the *Gazette* or the *Journal*. I even wanted to try to apply for writing for newsletters for trade organizations, just anything I could do to write, but it just didn't work."

Finally, through a contact, she found a job in the advertising department at the *Washington Post*. "I couldn't be in news because I didn't have any news experience. So they hired me as a sales aide in advertising. I used to traffic ads, you know, call them in, make space reservations, deal with the money. All that stuff. Well, I was set to move up in that too, but I really wanted to be in the newsroom. So I made a lateral move to the newsroom. So instead of answering phones in advertising, delivering faxes and all that, I started doing that in the newsroom. So I was there for another year and a half, during which time I had my baby. And I applied to the *Post*'s summer program, an internship with the six clips that I had to my name. In fact, I had to write one to get my sixth." Linda's persistence paid off. "And so I had a summer internship, I got the summer internship, and I was very successful. So they kept me on after that."

Rose Brody graduated from the University of Virginia in 1986 with a major in international relations and foreign affairs and set her sights on Capitol Hill in Washington, D.C. In her own words: "I said, 'Well, I really do want to work on Capitol Hill. How do I get there?' Well, I just went to the [federal] credit union and started working at the credit union, and on my breaks I would go upstairs and introduce myself to the staff or whatever. And then one day I had heard that there was an opening. I submitted my résumé. Up I went."

Robert Williams had the misfortune of graduating in 1992, at the tail end of the early '90s recession. Even with an engineering degree from Old Dominion, he said, "the market was so tight that I really didn't have a lot of opportunities to go on." He continued:

> I took my résumé and gave it to one of the contractors who were supporting the Navy that she [his wife] was working for. And this brother had my résumé and put it in, and you know I went in and interviewed and got the job. And I was only getting paid $21,000 a year. This was in '93, and this is an engineering . . . a junior engineering position. And I'm like, this makes no sense. It was a small, black-owned company. I knew the president, and I went to him, and I said I can't live off of $21,000 a year, not in this area. You know, I had an apartment and I was paying $590 a month. But you had to do what you had to do. And he gave me a raise, but it just wasn't where I needed to be. So I did the thing that everybody usually does, job hop. I'd spend a year and a half or two years on a job, and I would go. Every time, every step would be a progression. And it's always been government contracts around the federal government, but I took a job around the time we were getting ready to get married; I took a job at Martin

Marietta. I was working with a government agency, but I would work shifts. But my salary was doubled just by taking this job. I got a lot of good experience, and it was able to get me to where I am now.

While Robert's wife, Laura, who graduated with a BA in communications, did not have to "job hop" to find her desired job, her first job after college proved to be a long detour. It was a position she took during the tight market of the early 1990s that stretched out to seven long years. She reflected:

> So I worked for the Department of Navy, for First Naval Air Systems Command and then Strategic Systems Program, for a total of seven years. You couldn't have told me that I would, but I went, grew very quickly. I was a GS-13 when I left the government, and that was only after three years. The money was good, but I was so unhappy. I would drive to work saying, "I hate my job. I hate my job." I mean, that's what I would say, and I was like I have to catch myself. I'm like, "Oh, my God! I'm saying it out loud!" So I actually took a 50 percent pay cut when I went to BET [Black Entertainment Television]. That's how badly I wanted to leave what I was doing to get in the industry I wanted to be in.

THE 1980S AND 1990S

By the mid- to late 1980s and into the 1990s, the labor force had become more receptive to African American college graduates. This included the rapidly growing digital or "dot-com" economy. Evidence of this is the fact that in 1990 computer systems analyst had risen in the ranks to the seventh most common occupation among black male professionals and the twelfth ranked occupation among black female professionals. By 2000, computer systems analysts held first and fifth places among black professional males and females, respectively.

Several husbands and wives in my sample of sixty-two held jobs in the information technology (IT) industries. Some had majored in computer science as undergraduates, while others found their way to an IT job by chance. Kevin Tucker graduated from Morehouse with a major in computer science and was recruited by VPN. Fourteen years later, he continued at the same company. He spoke with pride and enthusiasm about his work in a company he said was "pioneering some new areas" and developing "leading-edge technologies." He added, "So I enjoy what I do. It's pretty good." Morris Gardner (whose wife landed her first journalism job in Peoria, Illinois), like Kevin Tucker, had an easy time trading his majors in math and computer science for an IT job. Contrasting her own job-hunting experience, Morris's wife, Karen, said that in Morris's case, job offers "just, like, rained on him." While not denying this, Morris provided a slightly different sequence. "I started with FEMA first. I had previously worked as an intern there, and when I graduated, when I left college, they offered me a job. Then after I started working there, that's when I started to get all the offers. I went to private industry and never went back."

While the IT industry is gendered in men's favor, several women in my sample also worked in IT. When I interviewed the Turners, Peggy had been working in the IT operational center of Lockheed Martin for four years, although her path to the IT industry had been more complicated than those of Morris Gardner and Kevin Tucker. After graduating with a degree in accounting, she assumed a position as an auditor at Arthur Andersen. She soon found IT was progressively changing what she did. As she explained, "IT was changing the way accountants audited. There was no longer a paper trail; it was an automated system trail. You have to know information technology in order to say that you can sign off on your financial statements. Because it changed my industry, I had to go back to school and become more familiar with the technology that was causing this shift in the field that I was working in. So that's primarily at the time why I went back to school and got a degree in information technology." Unlike her male counterparts in IT, the birth of her son and the subsequent demands of motherhood complicated Peggy's life. Her move to

Lockheed was in part to take advantage of the greater flexibility the company offered for combining work with motherhood.

Respondents found their first job in ways common to students generally. For some, like Morris Gardner and Jennifer Roberts, it came through an internship that turned into a regular position. Others, like John Berry and Laura Williams, were recruited on campus. A personal contact helped Steve Edwards: "My mom used to work at the NEA [National Education Association]." Likewise, for Christine Edwards, it was "somebody I knew." When asked how she found her first job, Rita Madison answered, "I got that on my own just by going through the *Washington Post* and sending out résumés." It was through his own search after coming out of the Marines that Alfred Henry also found his first job. "I went to an employment agency to search for a job and get some help. It happened pretty quickly. I think like a week or two—no, like a week. They placed me at Fannie Mae." Despite the diversity of ways they found their first job, the most common avenue to employment after college was through an internship or the traditional campus interview.

For most college graduates, the first job is the beginning of a long career that will evolve through many vertical and/or lateral moves. The common belief is that the typical career today will involve seven different jobs. No one knows the origin of this idea, which is disavowed by the Department of Labor Statistics. In my sample most husbands and wives had held three or four jobs by the time of my interview. Beyond the search for a first job and transitions to subsequent jobs, I explored the extent to which mentorships had affected their careers and whether they had encountered obstacles such as discrimination. I turn first to mentors.

Mentors

Mentors can smooth the way for young individuals new to the job market and for those entering a new position, regardless of age. Several interviewees made a point of stressing the importance of mentorship. When asked whether she had profited from mentors,

Betty Thomas replied, "Oh absolutely! Absolutely." Then she added, "Especially in corporate America, and in order to move up in a company you need to have somebody in a senior role who's gonna be your champion in order to get your foot in the door to compete." Laura Williams reflected on the importance of mentors in personal terms: "I definitely think it's so important in life to be coachable because we don't know everything. You couldn't have told me that coming out of college because I knew *everything*. I thought. But life will teach you that you really don't. So I really have learned to be coachable and be open for those mentors and even in finding someone that I would love to learn from, you know, to mentor."

About half of the men and slightly more than half of the women I interviewed acknowledged having had mentors. What did they learn from their mentors? How did mentors help them in their search for career mobility? Keith James described a mentor as "someone who's that confidant, someone who I can go to who's gonna guide me in the right direction, as far as giving me the advice that I need in the direction I should go." This was the kind of mentor Keith's wife, Sandra, had been fortunate to find early in her career in the federal government: "I was mentored when I was at a lower grade. And they were the ones that helped me get to the next, get to the higher levels. Mold me, tell me what I need to do, what courses I need to take, behaviors, you know. Don't be offended when people say this, don't do facial expressions, body language. So they kind of helped me ignore stuff."

Others spoke of the mentorships they received at different times in their careers. Joseph Howard could say, "The judge was a good mentor in my first job and then in my successive law firm jobs working in D.C. child/family services agencies. Everywhere I've gone I've picked up a mentor and still count on those folks for advice from time to time."

Likewise, Betty Thomas's career had profited from many mentors over the years. "I've had a lot of champions. Mostly African American women. I actually had a few white champions, or mentors, and one black male. In a variety of things. As an HR professional, as an attorney, and then, you know, little personal kinds of mentoring relationships that I've gained over the years."

Claudia Gilbert and Troy Roberts spoke of mentors as people who "showed me the ropes" or "helped me see the forest from the trees." Of her own mentor, Jennifer Roberts said, "She took me on board and under her tutelage. I learned quite a bit." Mary Douglas recounted the mentoring she received in two jobs. The first occurred while working in banking: "When I was in banking I did have someone who—she had been in banking for quite some time—and she was the one that kinda said, 'Hey, you know what? You can really move through the system because of having a degree.' And she kinda guided me up to a certain point, and then I was able to quickly advance. Yeah, I would say I had a mentor in banking."

Later when she moved to another job, the one she held at the time of our interview, she could say, "And so I did have someone who kinda brought me along, you know. She had been with the county for many years, and I kinda liked what she was doing, and she kinda brought me along, and it took off from there."

Edith Jamison explained the help she received as "just enforcing good work habits, discipline and getting stuff done; being organized, being fair, work distributed evenly. See this is the lady I was working behind, so I was very fortunate to be working under her. And in the beginning, working for the different men, I didn't care that much about my job. When I really started caring about it is when I was under this lady named Marie. And that's when I developed great work habits and how to be disciplined and organized. That was the main two things she emphasized."

Brian Thomas, who faced the daunting task of selling life insurance, had several mentors that he felt were "very helpful. Basically, they showed me that there is a market for black people to sell. Not a lot of black people sell financial services. There's no benefits and no vacation; there's none of that. It's hard. And he showed me that, one, you can do it, and there's a market for a black professional."

The impact of having a mentor was such that some individuals maintained a lasting relationship with their mentors. Julia Bell noted, "I'm still very close with my mentor now." Likewise, Joseph Howard could say, "Everywhere I've gone I've picked up a mentor too, and still count on those folks for advice from time to time."

While many women and men I interviewed had experienced very successful mentoring, this was not true for everyone. Among these individuals, a number spoke of their frustration. For Charles Brody, the lack of a mentor meant career opportunities lost. After earning an accounting degree, he quickly found a job in his field. He said, "I interviewed well, and I got into one of the firms. And I worked there for about three years, and there's a whole lot of things that happen when you start working in the accounting field." The lack of a mentor led him to conclude, "I probably would have done better if I had a mentor at that point."

Brad Hamilton, who "didn't [have a mentor] for the first ten years" of his career, later succeeded and could say during our interview, "Now I have great mentorship." Keith James, whose definition of mentoring I quoted above, was thinking of his own frustrations in finding a mentor. Reminiscing on the past, he commented, "As I moved through the ranks in corporate America I found it harder and harder for me to find a mentor who understood me. Understood some of the challenges I had. So that's why I found myself going outside. And that's not to say that I did not take advice; I did go to other people for advice. As I said, in each one of those positions as I moved up to be the only black that held that position, I found it very difficult to find that mentor. And I looked! I've spent several lunches, I've spent several meetings and sitting down and trying to pick that right person."

Like Charles Brody, who also worked in accounting, Peggy Turner had difficulty finding mentors. "I didn't have a lot. They were few and far in between. There weren't a lot of people who I would consider being my mentor because, you know, certain things I can't really compromise. I'm not that kind of person who would tell a client, 'Your financial statements look good,' when I *know* that they need work and we need to work on these financial statements. So I did find a few people here and there that I thought who gave me some good input, were my informal mentors, but none that I kept for twenty years."

For the majority of those who found mentors, the mentor's race was not an issue. Brad Hamilton, who had no mentor during his first ten years, commented on the question of the mentor's race. "I counsel a lot of young folks these days about mentorship and how to perceive their career. And it's foolish to think if you're black, you can go through and find only black mentors. It's foolish to find only white mentors. You just gotta be much more inclusive in that. So I probably have, you know, four folks that I call mentors, five, only one of them is black." Brad's experience was not unique. While a few women and men I interviewed had mentors of only one race or gender, they were the exception. More typical was the experience of Joseph Howard, who said that his mentors had been "a variety of people, white, black, men, women, Asian. All kinds of folks."

Workplace Discrimination

Movement up a career ladder is the goal of every middle-class worker and the reality that separates middle-class from working-class jobs. The success or failure of career upward mobility depends on many factors, objective and subjective. On the objective side, one can list human capital (education and skills), experience, performance on the job, and seniority. Subjective factors are more difficult to codify, as they include an individual's social and cultural capital, managers' tastes, prejudices, and actual discrimination. After the Civil Rights Act became law in 1964, recognizing the history of racial exclusion in the United States, Congress established the Equal Employment Opportunity Commission (EEOC) to monitor the legislation's ban on discrimination in employment and education. The law covers discrimination based on race, color, national origin, religion, sex, age, and disability, although the largest number of complaints appear to focus on racial and sex discrimination.

Much has changed since the Civil Rights Act in 1964. Overt discrimination has declined, while more subtle forms have increased. Since many recent articles and books have documented the continuation of workplace racial and sex discrimination, I wanted to discover the extent to which the men and women in my sample had been victims of racial discrimination. Around half of the husbands (seventeen) and wives (fifteen) acknowledged experiencing some type of workplace discrimination, from minor slights to denial of promotions or equal pay. However, discrimination is often difficult to prove or even to identify, as several respondents acknowledged.

Roy Bell expressed this dilemma in the following way: "The problem for black folk working in the predominately white environment is that if people have issues, what you first have to understand, try to discern, is whether it's because I'm black that I'm getting approached like this, or is it because the work that I have done. White folk, they know what it is; that it's the work." Roy's experience, however, was far from ambiguous, as he explained. "I would come in very competitive with my white counterparts and then come to find out after a couple of years, they were all ahead of me salary-wise. . . . Both of us in the same grade. This is like white males, even white females. They would come in lower than me, but somehow over the years, they tend to make more, maybe rewarded more with merit increases than I would, but yet I would have the major, the lion's share of the responsibility to keep everything going."

Charlene Johnson confirmed the ambiguity of African American workers when she spoke of her husband's experience as a salesman. "African American males, they're more descriptive, the way they move their hands; their presentation is not the same as that of a white male's. So, depending on who's looking on, they're not comfortable with the presentation. So I don't know what you call that, is it racism? Like at Dell, I don't think the white boys were comfortable with Alfred. I don't know if that's racism or what."

Despite the ambiguity, many times one would be hard-pressed to deny racism was involved. Promotion issues were most often mentioned. Typically, it was being passed over for a promotion or the hiring of someone white who was less senior or less qualified. Frank Harrison filed a discrimination suit and won.

FRANK: Yes, I filed a discrimination case at the Bureau of Engraving and Printing and won it.

LANDRY: What was it based on?

FRANK: Based upon race, based upon color. A white male, high school graduate, was promoted over me. And the selecting official was his neighbor in Virginia so I won the case. I got back pay, which went back almost a year, and I got promoted to GS-14. That was back in, oh God, 1994 at the Bureau of Engraving and Printing.

Frank had a bachelor's degree from the University of Maryland.

Frank's wife had a similar experience but did not file a discrimination suit. Charlene explained, "There was an opening last year as director of training that would train the entire mediator workforce. This person would develop training programs for our mediators, administer questionnaires, and deliver training to the field. And I figured who better to do that than me because I've been working there, I'm certified in training and development, I write most of their training programs they have now. But they hire a white man they didn't even know. So I said fine. You know, I just said, 'Well, if it's for me to get, I hope I get it, but if not . . .' Now the man is in there, and nobody likes him. And I'm like, 'Well, don't tell me.'"

Thomas Edison was also passed over for a position for which he was eminently qualified.

When my boss left, I had been doing everything associated with it [his job]. I mean I used to do the budget for our department—$15 million budget. So I did everything for the department. I was on call; like I said, all the hospitals called. So when I applied for the position, the medical director at the time was like, "Yeah." So it was assumed I would get this job. And we were going through the whole application process and doing three-level interviews. But in my second interview, one person says, "It's not my decision to make; it's his decision." When I'm at the third-level interview, this person says it's not his decision, it's her decision. Okay, so what does that mean? I already knew what that means. They got this person that had no background in it and then was failing.

Thomas's expectation was not unfounded. After he failed to be promoted to the position, several employees in the department came to him expressing their surprise. Remembering this experience, he said, "The director eventually came to me and said, 'I don't understand how you didn't get that job.' Then everyone keeps coming and saying, 'I don't understand.'"

Debbie Hamilton also faced workplace discrimination by being passed over for a position that one would have expected she would receive.

We were in a suburb of Chicago—Naperville, Illinois. In the bank, I would say there were probably 150 employees. Out of two African Americans, I was one of them. We worked in the same department. We worked on the consumer lending side. And she was an underwriter, and I was a processor/closer for consumer lending—car loans and personal loans. And we had my review, and my manager said: "Look, we're very happy with the work. The next underwriting slot, we'd like to promote you." I thought, okay, great, but I knew my girlfriend was leaving. So like a month after my review, she was gone. And immediately they hired someone else. And so I asked him outright , "Why did you overlook me? Is it because I'm black?" And he said, "So what if it is?" So we went through the legal department because of course I complained, and we went through the legal and it was really blown up, and they said, "We can't explain, oh we can't find any reason for you to think that you were overlooked because of this." Went on for a month. And then all of a sudden, the department was reorganized, and I was put into the mortgage side, which was the processor/closer title but you did processing, closing, underwriting, which was the same grade as the underwriter on the consumer side. So it was kind of interesting, but I went through that.

LANDRY: So the person that told you "What if it is?" I assume this was a different person than the one who said you would get the job.

DEBBIE: He was her manager, my manager's manager.

Salary was the other frequently mentioned area of workplace discrimination. Like promotion discrimination, salary discrimination was often blatant, as in David George's case. "The majority of folks that I brought in, came in at probably like $5,000 to $10,000 more than I was making. No more education than I had, but they weren't the same color I was. And then I learned this through talking to a lot of them who said, 'Well, I make this.' And I was, okay, interesting. So after I heard this from three or four people, I went to my boss. I said, 'You got me training these guys who are learning from me but yet apparently you think they're better than me, because you're paying them more. How do I get my salary on par with them?' 'You're not supposed to be discussing salary' was the reply. 'Well, it's out there now. What are you going to do about it?'"

Steve Edwards had a similar experience of blatant salary discrimination. "The job before my last job, the reason I left was because my manager one day sent out this e-mail, and he attached everybody's salary; and I notice that my salary was the lowest. I was the only black person that worked there, but I was selling more than anybody else. And I approached him about it, and he said, 'Well, there's nothing I can do about it.' The company was in the state of Virginia. I wanted to sue him so bad, but I talked to a couple lawyers and they said unless he calls you an N, there's really nothing you can do. So I just left."

Beyond the more tangible losses of income and promotion, many respondents complained about the less tangible problems of workplace climate, including isolation, stress, and feelings of marginalization. Several voiced the old adage that a black person must work "twice as hard" as a white employee. Andrew White complained of having "to do it twice as good to get half as far." With obvious strong feelings of frustration, Andrew, who traveled extensively providing technical service for his company, described his stressful experiences.

ANDREW: So most of the time, 90 percent of the time, when I show up, last name Ireland, black face, that's always a surprise, number one. Then number two I spend unnecessary time trying to prove myself before I'm given the opportunity to do what I'm hired to do. So it's always been a real struggle, a real challenge. I'm always challenged, I'm questioned, and it's been a battle; and I think I've done well despite that. But it gets old to have to go to work with gloves on all the time.

BRENDA: It's stressful.

ANDREW: It's very stressful. But I don't care how you look at it or what kind of person you are, after so many situations it tends to make you feel a certain way. I don't deserve that. All I did was walk in. You hired my company; I'm representing my company. They sent me because I'm qualified to do this service, and it's pretty tough.

Andrew's wife, Brenda, who was born when the Civil Rights Act was passed, explained how hitting "brick walls" for twenty years had changed her.

I don't want to be president; I'm past the age of being president. I just want privacy now; leave me alone. Let me do my things, let me live my life, take my vacations, whatever. Give me a paycheck. Not to say that I'm not motivated and I don't want to do a good job. But my focus has changed, and part of changing my focus has been constantly hitting a brick wall. So I've been like, "Well, forget it. I'll go a different direction to seek that satisfaction." And I think a lot of black people do that. Especially our age. You get tired of hitting the brick walls, and then, you know, some people come back and say, "Oh, you're not motivated, and you're not this." It's like, well I was motivated for twenty years. You weren't listening, and you were beating me down. And now, I do a good job, but now, I've actually turned down opportunities at my job, because I don't want those positions now that are going to require me to work at home and do this and do that.

Some female respondents recounted the difficulty they experienced receiving recognition by male colleagues. Betty Thomas reported, "I have always been, well not always, but most instances the only black woman at the table. And usually dealing with an opposing counsel, 'cause we're dealing with a corporate issue. I'm representing my company, he's representing his company, and sometimes they just have preconceived ideas of who you are based on how you look. And then even dealing with people on your own side, there's always me and a lot of white male counterparts in the room. And you can sometimes feel invisible because they will attempt to talk around you or keep you out of the conversation. So you literally have to exert a lot more energy to be heard and to be a part of the team."

Margaret Francis had similar experiences of lack of recognition due to preconceptions of gender and race. She described it as getting "the look."

She micromanaged us, managed us to death. She was a white woman who had, she had some serious issues. She, she was the woman I told my husband when I came home, I said I got the *look*. You know the look, like yes we do have a brain, yes we can go to college, yes we can be successful, yes we can be—you know. It's the look where they're surprised to see you. That look, I'll never forget it. My first job [as a physician assistant] in Virginia—Dulles, Virginia. I was at United Airlines. Same look.

They were all white men. When I came into the board room, I was second in charge. Some of them wouldn't even look at me. And that was in 1990. I was kind of crushed. I called my father. I was quite upset. He said, "Did you run the meeting?" I said, "I ran it." He said, "Did you finish it?" Yeah. He said, "Are you starting to cry?" 'Cause I'm in my office by myself. I was very young, I was right out of Howard, and I was sort of, you know, idealistic about them accepting us, so to speak.

Later, when I asked if she had experienced any other discrimination, she replied, "No. I've always just gotten that look." She added sadly, "I hate to be pessimistic. I don't think it will ever change."

After describing a discriminatory event of the past, Charlene Johnson spoke of her current work experience in a primarily white environment. "So now, it's not discrimination. It's just working with white people; it's different. It's just different. They just don't want you to be smarter than them. That's what I think. I don't know how else to put it. They don't want a black person to be smarter than them."

Middle-class black professionals have increased significantly in numbers, have entered a far greater range of occupations than in the past, and have attained what is considered the American Dream. Yet the shadow of discrimination haunts them, as half of the husbands and wives attest to experiencing racial and/or gender discrimination. Upward mobility into the middle class provides no antidote against discrimination. Formerly, the attainment process ended with an individual's entry into the labor market to claim his or her position in the class structure. Position in the class structure, as Weber suggests, provides the resources for one's life chances or standard of living. These resources include a package of income and benefits that are used for constructing a living standard and the accumulation of wealth. In the next chapter, I turn to the growth of income and wealth among middle-class blacks and whites and their analysis in the thirty-one couples in my sample.

8
Income and Wealth

Although class position is not defined by income, income is one of the most important ingredients of the compensation package attached to one's job. It is income, with benefits such as health insurance, paid sick leave, and retirement programs, that determines a worker's "life chances" (in Max Weber's term) or standard of living. The significance of holding a middle-class job—especially an upper-middle-class job—is the size, content, and stability of the compensation "package" attached to the job. The larger the compensation package, the higher the potential living standard accessible. The quality of one's house, neighborhood, children's education, health care, and leisure consumption are all outcomes of the compensation package attached to your job.

As I discussed earlier in chapter 6, in Max Weber's attainment model a person's class is determined by position in the labor (or commodity) market, while position in the labor market itself depends on the skill or education level brought to the market during entry. Attainable life chances result from the individual's position (job) in the labor market.

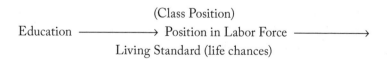

(Class Position)

Education ⟶ Position in Labor Force ⟶

Living Standard (life chances)

The higher the education or skill level, therefore, the higher the class position potentially attainable, and the higher the living standard. The most accessible statistics, however, connect only the first two stages: education and income.

Wealth is also important for supporting living standards but is secondary to income since most workers' wealth holdings are modest and in the form of home ownership. In recent decades tapping the equity in one's home with an equity loan has become a popular means of increasing income for immediate consumption, be it for financing children's education, home repairs, or a vacation. Banks' encouragement of this practice indicates that it also increases indebtedness and profits for them. While often helpful in increasing one's consumption, it is not a free ride. Home ownership, therefore, falls under the heading of wealth for *personal use.*

Stocks and bonds are *productive* wealth, wealth that generates more income without the necessity of labor. This form of wealth is heavily concentrated in the upper class and has in recent decades led to a large increase in income inequality in the United States and other countries. Still, stock ownership has spread among workers since the stock market boom of the 1990s, reaching a peak of 65 percent of U.S. adults in 2007, according to Gallup. The subsequent decline in the rate of stock ownership to 52 percent in 2013 has occasioned much speculation and hand-wringing in the press. According to Gallup, this decline was broad-based among workers across all age and income groups. The Gallup statistics include ownership of individual stocks, mutual funds, and self-directed 401(k)s and IRAs. Since, according to the *2014 Investment Company Fact Book*, the majority (92 percent) of mutual fund investors do so for retirement, this form of wealth holding does not increase worker-investors' daily living standard. For most workers, therefore, their living standard is a consequence of the compensation received from their position in the class structure.

Black Middle-Class Income

As in the previous chapters, I first look at the national picture for a broader understanding of the income and wealth of middle-class African Americans. Afterward, I examine income and wealth within my interviewed sample. The story of income at the national level over the past decade has not been encouraging. According to the *Federal Reserve Bulletin* and other reports, in recent years families in the middle range of the income distribution have seen little or no increase in average incomes, and those at the lower range suffered losses. Only those families at the top have made significant gains. Although some of the losses and stagnation have resulted from the recent economic downturn and recession, the long-term trend has been an increase in income and wealth inequality in the United States. Against this background, I analyze income and wealth in the African American middle class.

I first compare black and white incomes using income quintiles and then move to a comparison of the income of specific occupational groups within the middle class. Income quintiles (the division of the national income into five categories ranked from low to high) is a favorite tool of economists. While sociologists view quintiles as income groups and not classes, a study of quintiles across racial groups can yield important insights. What can we learn from income quintiles? Dividing the national income or the income of a particular group and ranking the groups from the highest to the lowest quintile offers a quick view of the level of inequality in the nation or group. (See Figure 8.1.)

The extent of national income inequality is clearest from an inspection of the top and bottom fifths of the income distribution. In 2013, the top or fifth quintile (20 percent) of all families owned 49 percent of all family income in the nation. The bottom fifth had only 4 percent, while the top 5 percent alone commanded 21 percent of all family income. One must go back to the post–World War II period until the late 1970s to find a more equitable income distribution, "more equitable" being a euphemism that

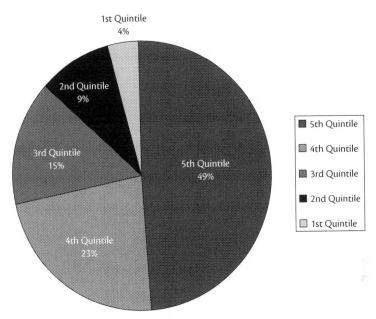

1st Quintile
4%

2nd Quintile
9%

3rd Quintile
15%

5th Quintile
49%

4th Quintile
23%

5th Quintile
4th Quintile
3rd Quintile
2nd Quintile
1st Quintile

FIG. 8.1. Share of Aggregate National Income by Each Fifth, All Families
Source: U.S. Census, historical income tables, Families Table F-2, 2013.

refers to a slightly more equal income distribution. In 1974, the
bottom quintile owned 6 percent of the national income, compared to 4 percent in 2013; the fifth quintile owned 41 percent
rather than 49 percent in 2013, and the top 5 percent owned
15 percent. The second, third, and fourth quintiles owned 9, 15,
and 23 percent, respectively, in 1974. National income inequality
has progressively increased since 1974.

Income Distribution between Black and White Families

Except for some minor differences, the income distributions of
blacks and whites, as measured by quintiles, closely mirror the
national profile. The top quintile among whites owned 47 percent
of *white income* in 2013, while the bottom quintile accounted for
only 5 percent. Their top 5 percent had 21 percent of all white
income. (See Figure 8.2.) The black quintile distribution showed

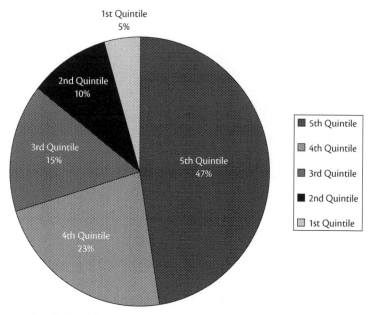

1st Quintile
5%

2nd Quintile
10%

3rd Quintile
15%

4th Quintile
23%

5th Quintile
47%

- 5th Quintile
- 4th Quintile
- 3rd Quintile
- 2nd Quintile
- 1st Quintile

FIG. 8.2. Share of Aggregate Group Income by Each Fifth, All White Families
Source: U.S. Census, historical income tables, Families Table F-2, 2013.

somewhat higher inequality within the black community, with the fifth quintile commanding 51 percent of *black income*, and the first or lowest quintile owning only 3 percent—a consequence of the higher rate of poverty among blacks. The top 5 percent held 22 percent of black family income. (See Figure 8.3.)

While quintiles are not classes, it is reasonable to assume that at least a large percentage of the middle classes can be found somewhere within the top two quintiles, the fourth and fifth. Without occupational information we cannot determine how they are distributed across these two quintiles. With the above assumption, we can gain insight into income differences between black and white middle-class families by comparing the mean (or average) income of the two top quintiles. In 2013, the mean of the top (fifth) white quintile was $212,080, compared to $151,525 for blacks, while the means of the fourth quintiles were $100,542 and $68,601

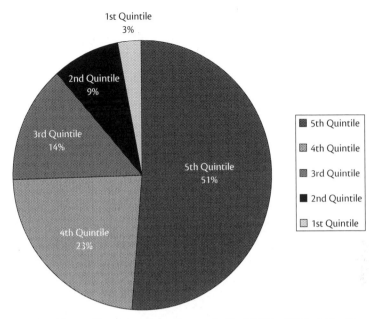

1st Quintile
3%

2nd Quintile
9%

3rd Quintile
14%

5th Quintile
51%

4th Quintile
23%

5th Quintile
51%

- 5th Quintile
- 4th Quintile
- 3rd Quintile
- 2nd Quintile
- 1st Quintile

FIG. 8.3. Share of Aggregate Group Income by Each Fifth, All Black Families
Source: U.S. Census, historical income tables, Families Table F-2, 2013.

for whites and blacks, respectively. These are striking differences that reveal large gaps in the income holdings of middle-class blacks and whites.

For more detailed comparisons of middle-class black and white *individual* incomes, I turn to specific occupational groups within the middle class. I make these comparisons for the years 2010 and 2013, when the occupational data are comparable. As in the previous comparisons, I show only the averages since, unlike the median, the average is sensitive to the highs and lows of groups and I expect there are more whites at the higher income level than blacks.

In chapter 7, I discussed the distribution of blacks and whites in the professional stratum of the middle class.[1] The largest category is "professional and related occupations." Below this broad group, we find many subgroups. In 2010, the mean income for all blacks in the professional and related occupations stratum was

$55,304, compared to $72,971 for whites, a difference of over $17,000. By 2013, the difference had increased to slightly over $18,000 ($59,092 to $77,368).

Since males and females hold different occupations, I compare occupational groups known to have a higher concentration of males or females. In chapter 7, I noted that black professionals were not only diversifying but also entering important new fields like computers. The census category for this area includes computer scientists, analysts, programmers, engineers, and administrators. In 2010 black males holding these jobs earned an average of $57,754. By 2013, their average income had climbed to $71,939. White males, already at a mean of $83,861 in 2010, saw a rise to $85,445 by 2013. While these figures might seem low for this industry, they are averages, with many earning more as well as less. Not all programmers and workers in the computer industry are employees in Silicon Valley. In the male-dominated field of engineering, white males again were much higher earners than black males in 2013, with respective income averages of $87,293 for blacks and $99,540 for whites.

Elementary and high school teaching is a profession that both blacks and whites have long held and one where women are concentrated. Before the passage of the Civil Rights Act, black teachers were confined to working in segregated black schools. Civil rights legislation opened the doors of all-white schools where teachers earned higher salaries. The average income for black female teachers in elementary and secondary jobs was $40,350 in 2010 and had only risen to $41,891 by 2013. White female teachers had income means about $7,000 higher in both 2010 ($47,660) and 2013 ($49,376). Nurses earn average salaries higher than teachers, but here again white females outearned black females by almost $5,000 on average in 2010 ($54,589 to $59,348) and by over $8,000 in 2013 ($54,123 to $62,522). While the income average for black female nurses slipped by 2013, the average for white female nurses climbed by several thousand dollars.

Black and White Wealth: A Comparison

A comparison of the wealth holdings of blacks and whites faces the same obstacle as a comparison of incomes.[2] Wealth statistics rarely include the occupations needed for Weberian class analysis. One of the most useful published analyses of wealth by race comes from a study by Sharmila Choudhury, who analyzed wealth by income *quartiles* for blacks, whites, and Latinos.[3] To use her results for my own racial comparisons, I follow the same approach as above with income quintiles.

Wealth includes different financial and tangible assets. Tangible assets comprise vehicles, business assets, other property of value, and an individual's or family's primary residence. Financial assets include stocks and bonds, retirement accounts such as IRAs and Keogh plans, and checking and savings accounts. How do these wealth holdings vary across black and white middle-class families? Since wealth includes a great variety of assets, comparative results depend on which of these assets are included. It also depends on the construction of the comparison groups. Comparing all blacks with all whites is unrealistic since the class distribution of blacks and whites differs markedly, with a higher percentage of whites at the upper end and a higher percentage of blacks at the lower end. There is a higher percentage of upper-middle-class whites and a higher percentage of working-class blacks, although there are blacks and whites in all classes. Comparing across specific classes yields more accurate findings.

The study by Sharmila Choudhury uses data from the 1992 Health and Retirement Study, a survey that covers individuals near retirement at the time of the survey. Given the difficulty of finding adequate wealth data, and especially wealth data that also contains individual occupations, I am using Choudhury's study to offer a *rough* comparison of wealth between the black and white middle classes before analyzing my own qualitative interview data. There is a difference in the wealth holdings of the upper class and the wealth holdings of the middle and working classes. Upper-class wealth, which includes the assets of over

440 billionaires, is concentrated in financial, industrial, and real estate assets. The wealth of middle-class individuals and families is far more modest.

To use Choudhury's data for racial comparisons of wealth holdings, I assume that a high percentage of upper-middle-class blacks and whites are found in the highest quartile of the data reported in her analysis. I begin with housing equity since this is the most important of the assets owned by middle-class individuals and families. Although an almost identical percentage of whites and blacks in Choudhury's highest quartile owned homes in 1992 (100 to 99.01 percent), the average house value differed drastically: $551,818 to $250,028 for whites and blacks, respectively. Using this approximation for the middle class yields an average black middle-class housing value in 1992 that was 45 percent that of whites. Since a percentage of even near retirees still carry a mortgage, the real housing wealth is the equity in the house. A smaller percentage of both whites and blacks owned equity in their homes (98 percent and 89 percent), which could result from second mortgages or newly purchased homes. In 1992, average black middle-class housing equity (those in the highest income quartile) was about 70 percent of the average white housing equity: $81,110 to $116,441. A comparison of average housing equity for blacks and whites of all four quartiles combined yielded a mean of $70,621 for whites compared to $29,656 for blacks, or 42 percent of white housing equity in 1992. These lower figures for all individuals, regardless of class, confirm the importance of comparisons across the same class for greater accuracy. These housing statistics are only for individuals' primary home.

Financial Wealth

Of the various forms of financial wealth, I compare stocks, bonds, and retirement assets. In 1992, stock ownership by members of the fourth quartile of this preretirement group was 56 percent for whites, close to the 52 percent found by Gallup for the nation in 2013. In 1992, the percentage of stock-owning blacks in the highest quartile was slightly less than half that of whites at 26 percent. The average values of stocks owned by the two groups were also lopsided: $102,958 and $54,258, or a black ownership value of slightly more than half (53 percent) of white ownership value. Relatively few individuals venture into the bonds market. In this sample, only 16 percent of whites and 5 percent of blacks in the fourth quartile owned bonds.

Unlike stocks and bonds, retirement accounts can be viewed as deferred wealth rather than wealth available for present use. They represent an individuals' attempt to secure their future living standard. For the middle class, retirement accounts represent their best hope of maintaining their current living standard. The principal financial assets for retirement are Social Security and employment pension accounts. Over the past decades, the traditional pension that was tied to a single employer with whom a worker spent his or her lifelong career has morphed into a dizzying variety of individual, employer, and government plans, each with its own regulations. The most familiar retirement assets are 401(k)s, IRAs, and Keoghs. Typically, both employer and employee contribute monthly to only 401(k). Choudhury presents data for Social Security, IRAs, and Keoghs.

It can be argued that Social Security is the most egalitarian of retirement accounts since everyone who works must pay into the account and receive contributions from their employer. Variance arises from the size of the contributions, which increase with workers' salaries and by type of occupation. The egalitarian character of Social Security is apparent from the almost equal percentages of black and white individuals in the fourth quartile receiving this benefit (97 percent and 97.6 percent). Differences in the average values of the benefits—$165,353 to $148,298—reveal an inherent unequal feature of Social Security as a wealth-building instrument.

Data from the Health and Retirement Study told a different story for wealth building through IRAs and Keoghs, which Choudhury analyzes together. Far more whites (72 percent) than blacks (44 percent) in the fourth quartile reported owning IRAs and

Keoghs, perhaps due to differences in public- versus private-sector employment and/or personal preferences for retirement options. For blacks who owned IRAs and Keoghs, however, the average dollar values were very similar to those of whites: $64,241 to $63,075, respectively, a suggestion that blacks who choose these retirement options are as successful as whites in wealth building through this means. This may reflect a similar use of these instruments and perhaps the similar incomes of those who do.

What do we learn from this limited analysis of wealth building by black and white middle-class individuals? First, the discussion of Choudhury's research suggests that any global statement of the difference between black and white wealth accumulation is misleading, given their unequal class distributions. It is far more accurate to compare black and white wealth differences across the same classes. Despite data problems, such as the lack of occupational information, approximations of wealth using the highest quartile suggest several conclusions. The racial wealth gap between upper-middle-class blacks and whites varies by the tangible or financial asset measured. Home ownership, the most important wealth held by anyone below the upper class, should be analyzed for both market value and equity in the home.

According to Choudhury's analysis of data from the 1992 Health and Retirement Study, a racial gap of 21 percent in home ownership between blacks and whites in the lowest quartile disappears between blacks and whites in the highest (fourth) income quartile (100 percent to 99.01 percent). The gap is only 3 percent in the third quartile. Within the upper middle class, therefore, the housing wealth gap is not in ownership but in market value and equity. For those at the fifth quartile level, the market value of black homes is 45 percent that of white homes, while the equity in black homes is 70 percent that of white homes. As we move down the class ladder, blacks and whites, but especially blacks, own homes of lower market value.

The largest racial wealth gap was in financial assets, in both ownership and value. White stock ownership in 1992 (56 percent) was close to the level found by Gallup for the nation in 2013

(52 percent), or around half of all adults. Far fewer upper-middle-class white individuals and families had financial wealth in stocks than in homes. While black upper-middle-class home ownership was at the same level as whites, the gap in stock ownership was large: 56 percent to 26 percent, or about 46 percent of white stock ownership. If we compare the stock valuation of only stock *owners*, the gap is somewhat less than 50 percent: $102,958 to $54,258. Still, the important questions are why so few upper-middle-class blacks own stocks and why their stocks are valued at only about half that of whites.

We can ask a similar question about ownership of IRAs and Keoghs. Choudhury found that black ownership of these two retirement instruments was 60 percent that of whites (72 percent to 44 percent)—better than stock ownership but still lagging considerably. Here the surprise is that the average values of IRAs and Keoghs owned by blacks and whites in the fifth quartile were equal: $63,075 for whites and $64,241 for blacks. The inequality gap in this form of financial wealth is in the level of ownership but not value.

Some researchers have suggested that blacks are more averse than whites to investing in risky assets such as stocks. If this is true, perhaps even successful blacks feel less secure economically. Middle-class blacks are more likely than whites to be first-generation college graduates and may also feel less secure in their employment because of discrimination. As a result, they may be less inclined to venture into the stock market than the housing market.

What do we learn about comparative racial income and wealth from this analysis? We learn that income at the national level and between classes for both blacks and whites is significantly unequal. Group-level inequalities are reflected in income inequality at the occupational levels. In spite of significant progress since 1964, black middle-class families and individuals still lag seriously behind whites of the same class level. Racial wealth inequality patterns follow closely those in income. However, greater understanding of racial wealth inequality is gained from comparisons across different assets and across the same class than from global comparisons of blacks versus whites.

I turn now to my own interview data, which may yield answers to some of these questions.

A Closer Look at Black Income and Wealth: The Prince George's County Sample

When I interviewed the thirty-one black upper-middle-class couples of Prince George's County in 2007, most had been in the labor force for decades and had experienced considerable career mobility. Some spoke of an earlier time in their careers and marriages when they earned much less. As their work careers matured, rising incomes allowed them to improve their living standards. Typically, it was only after several moves that they arrived in a solid upper-middle-class black neighborhood in South Bowie or some other growing middle-class area of the county. The purchase of a home in one of these new neighborhoods solidified their position in the upper middle class and represented a significant increase in their wealth holdings.

As the discussion earlier in this chapter suggests, wealth accumulation unfolds over a lifetime as individuals and families acquire material and financial assets. I begin with the most important of material assets for those individuals and families below the upper class: a home. The initial purchase conveys a mortgage and little equity. For most, that initial purchase, no matter how modest, begins the process of wealth accumulation that evolves over several moves across many decades. For the thirty-one families I interviewed, settling in Prince George's County stretched from 1979 to 2004, across several economic periods that included two recessions and an economic boom in the 1990s. During this period, both the class and racial composition of the county changed dramatically. From a predominantly white working-class and lower-middle-class county, Prince George's became a county with a large black upper middle class. Racially, the county's composition went from 37 percent black in 1980 to 63 percent black by 2000. Against this background, I analyze wealth accumulation in the housing market by upper-middle-class blacks in Prince George's County. By the time I interviewed them in 2007, the thirty-one couples were living in homes valued at $500,000 to $750,000. For most, it had been a decades-long journey to reach this point.

The Gilbert family is a good example of this process of material wealth accumulation. Their process began in 1983 in Des Moines, Iowa, where they owned a home valued at $50,000. Sticker shock awaited them upon their arrival in the Washington, D.C., metro area. Like many other families who moved into Prince George's County, they discovered, in the words of Claudia Gilbert, that "all we could afford was really at that time a townhouse." The next year they moved into a brand-new townhouse in Kettering that cost $100,000. Four years later, they responded to a Realtor's appeal and moved to a larger home in Upper Marlboro. The price tag: $140,000. When I interviewed them nineteen years later in 2007, the same house had quadrupled in value to $560,000, resulting in a significant increase in equity wealth.

Jennifer and Troy Robert, who began their life together in Prince George's County in a rented apartment in 1986, four years later bought their first townhouse in Mitchellville for $115,000. Troy explained, "We were in an apartment in Mount Rainier, so we were looking to stop renting and [buy]. So we moved into a townhome. We bought a townhome in Mitchellville." Six years later, in 1996, after looking at nearby counties, they moved to a new house on a one-acre lot with a price tag just under $300,000. It was a new subdivision, in a part of Prince George's County that was growing rapidly. Sensing an opportunity, developers created new communities that proved very attractive to upper-middle-class blacks seeking to raise their living standards with the purchase of new, larger homes. For Jennifer and Troy, buying the first house in the cul-de-sac, even before it was built, proved to be a good financial move into a neighborhood whose housing value was soon to appreciate substantially. By 2007, the market value of their home had more than doubled.

Several families settled directly into a black upper-middle-class neighborhood and were still in the same house in 2007. The Bells who moved from Boston in 1989 bought a house for $189,000 in the King's Forest development in Bowie. It was a house that Roy explained had "an office, family room, dining room and everything. So it was like the top of the line in this area." When I interviewed them in 2007, a similar house across the street was priced at $500,000. The Brookses also settled directly into a black upper-middle-class neighborhood in Bowie that fit their criteria. "We had a realtor," Denise Books explained, "and this is where they pointed us and we liked it. It was smaller, the things that we were looking for in the subdivision was a smaller subdivision. We didn't feel comfortable with the one across the street because that one was three times the size of this. We weren't looking for all those amenities. I'm from the south, so I wanted to have a more traditional, stable environment, not where people are coming and going a lot. And we thought this might be it." Their purchase cost $225,000 in 1996 and was valued about twice that in 2007.

Wealth building through home ownership is a cultural value in the United States. The federal government has encouraged it since the post–World War II period through such programs as FHA and VA mortgages that require small down payments and a guarantee against non-payment. As we saw above, home ownership among upper-middle-class blacks and whites has been about 100 percent. In 2010, the national rate for home ownership for all households was 66.9 percent, a figure that varied appreciably by race and ethnicity: whites 74.4, blacks 45.4, Hispanic 47.5. The message is clear: the upper middle class–black or white–is more successful in material wealth accumulation.

Caveats about Home Ownership Wealth

There are caveats when considering wealth accumulation through home ownership. Although important, home ownership wealth lacks the flexibility of financial wealth that can be bought and sold almost at will. Home ownership is "encumbered wealth" in that, if it is the owner's primary residence (wealth for personal use), it is restricted to its use as a domicile. (Second homes and investment property do not have the same restrictions.) The equity can be tapped to meet expenses such as education but that generates further debt of a second mortgage. It is also inheritable wealth. The homeowners I interviewed recognized that home ownership wealth was limited.

First, like the stock market, there is market fluctuation. Despite reaping a four-fold gain in market value, Dennis Gilbert was sanguine about the gain, noting: "The housing market is starting to slide." In 2007, they were nearing the housing crisis and recession that would erode housing values and equity. By 2007, the housing market was drastically different from the time they purchased their home. They had been fortunate to buy in the 1990s when a strong economy lifted most boats. In 2007, Claudia realized that the calculations were very different. It had become a different, far more expensive housing market. In response to my question about moving, she replied, "I'm not thinking of leaving. It doesn't make any sense to sell our house for three times, four times than what we paid for it, 'cause that's what it's been appraised for, and then go buy a place for much more than what this is worth. And do what, I mean, at our age?" Troy Roberts also recognized the difficulty of more housing wealth growth in the changing market. "Could I move, sell? Sure I could sell, but then I gotta spend a lot more money to get what I got now. I'm not looking to downsize. Just even take a lateral, get something similar, will cost me three times as much." Both families had gained considerable material wealth in the housing markets of the 1990s and early 2000s. Now they were in a holding position rather than looking forward to further growth.

Still, black middle-class families who settled in Bowie and some other parts of Prince George's County in recent decades experienced an enviable increase in their housing wealth. The post-2008 housing crisis and recession eroded some of this wealth, as it did in communities across the United States. However, with home ownership, as in the stock market, there is always the likelihood that values will again rise in these upscale communities. Home ownership remains one of the most important wealth generators for individuals and families. The Prince George's County case also points to important issues in the accumulation of housing wealth: location and timing.

The counterintuitive acquisition of significant housing wealth by middle-class blacks in mostly black communities resulted from a combination of chance occurrences: a period of rapid economic growth beginning in the late 1980s that continued through the 1990s and early 2000s and the development of upscale communities in a racially changing area of Prince George's County. It is an anomaly for a community undergoing racial transition (i.e., white flight) to experience rising property values. Historically, it has always been the opposite. As numerous studies have revealed, middle-class blacks often have difficulties entering wealthy neighborhoods because of cost or real or perceived discrimination. The results are racialized neighborhoods with housing of unequal market value and consequently unequal opportunities for wealth acquisition.

Many of my respondents emphasized that one of their motives for purchasing a house in Prince George's County was gaining "more bang for the buck," a superior housing value than they could find for the same money in one of the neighboring counties. In making what was without doubt a rational and logical choice at the time, they were also bypassing an opportunity for more wealth creation over time. As many couples also noted, given the poor quality of the public school system in Prince George's County, they were compelled to spend a considerable amount on private schools, expenses that would not have been necessary in one of the neighboring counties with high-performing public schools. Also, a house in neighboring counties would likely appreciate more over time than the same house in Prince George's County. These negatives were a surprise to some who did not yet have school-aged children when they first bought a home there; to others, it represented a weighing of the pluses and minuses involved in any major purchase. Finally, it would seem that middle-class blacks have more negatives to consider in finding affluent neighborhoods than middle-class whites and face more obstacles to housing wealth creation.

Stocks and Investment Property

To place stock investment in perspective, we must remember that widespread investment in the stock market is relatively new. For the general public, it can be traced to the late 1990s and early 2000s, when a rising stock market and dot-com boom created hundreds of tech millionaires who captured daily headlines. Soon centers for day-trading were springing up in large cities, beckoning the unwary investor eager to capitalize on the market boom. For a few this became an opportunity for a windfall, while for many more it was an "opportunity" to lose hard-earned savings. Still, investing in the stock market had taken hold, and increasing numbers of middle-class Americans entered the stock market. Prior to this period, one looked to the traditional passbook savings account to sock away income for a rainy day, for children's college, or for retirement. As recently as the early 1980s, anyone could score an interest rate of up to 10 percent on a passbook savings account at a bank or a savings and loan. By the end of the 1980s, as the country emerged from the deepest recession in the postwar era, these interest rates were rapidly dropping while interest rates on loans were rising. The traditional investment vehicle for working Americans was fast disappearing. Because of this historical background, it is easy to understand why a booming stock market became attractive to millions.

One other avenue for wealth creation was within reach for the middle class: buying investment property. This was especially popular among African Americans. In an insecure world, many black families sought security in the ownership of land or homes. The tradition began in the South, where most African Americans lived, and moved North with black migration to the industrial cities in search of employment and a life free of the daily indignities of segregation. Not surprisingly, over half of the thirty-one families I interviewed owned investment property. Kevin Tucker, who affirmed he preferred property to stocks, alluded to his father's admonition as his motivation. "My father told me: 'Buy some land somewhere, and it'll always work for you.' So I'm a firm believer in that. I'd like to own investment properties more so than anything else. Because it accrues in value, and you can sell it or you have a lot of options there." While Kevin did not own investment property, he emphasized that he and his wife were "looking" to buy real properties.

In my conversation with Troy and Jennifer Roberts, it became evident that, like the Tuckers, they too had the example of their parents to point the way.

LANDRY: Any investment, property or stocks?

JENNIFER: Just in the 401(k), stocks in the 401(k). Not outside of that.

LANDRY: No property?

JENNIFER: No. Something we've thought about doing, but haven't made means to put it in the budget because of the private school thing. So once we lift that burden, that'll free us up. We've thought about getting property in Florida. He wants to go get a place down there, just to rent and stuff. My parents actually own a property in Myrtle Beach. And my father has owned homes throughout Baltimore City. So it's there [the motivation], but we don't have the means to quite do that yet. So it's something that my dad has done. He's owned four or five properties at any given time. With him being older now and retired, he has sold off all the Baltimore properties and made handsomely. Like I said, it'll be money there to finance the grandchildren's college. But he has, he still has his property in Myrtle Beach.

While Troy and Jennifer did not yet have "the means" to buy investment property, many others did and had already invested. Sometimes the motive was securing money for a child's college. The Johnsons, who were saving for their daughter's college through a 529 college saving plan, had also bought a house for the same purpose. They explained: "As it appreciates and in ten years when she graduates, then we'll use that house or we'll sell it." Likewise, the Howards owned a house they rented in the city where their daughter attended college. Joseph Howard explained, "It's mainly for the students down in North Carolina, so hopefully we can keep students running through there." Frances added, "She [their daughter] lives in it with two roommates. And we will hopefully leverage that with some other properties either there or somewhere else." The Harringtons, who had owned several houses "in New Orleans off and on," turned to the same strategy as the Howards: "We bought instead of putting our daughter in a dorm, we just bought her a condo. Same price; less actually."

I heard stories of success similar to that of Peggy Turner, who retained the condominium she bought while in graduate school and was now renting it. "I rent it out and then use the money to pay the mortgage." Kay Berry, on the other hand, lamented that she and her husband had not acted similarly. "If we were savvier when we bought this house, we would have held on to our other one. Then we would have had a nice piece of appreciation." "So, we're looking," John added. "I'm looking at stuff right now actually." There were also those who had rather ambitious plans. This was the case with the Whites. Brenda White explained their strategy: "We actually took a more aggressive approach because we felt like we were behind, and life happens and you don't always have all the money to put aside that you want. So we started a couple of years ago investing in property, and our plan was to buy basically four houses. One for each year, and sell one every year. And we bought two last year, and thus far it's working. Because in less than one year we have maybe $40,000 worth of equity on one and probably about $25,000 or $30,000 on the other. That's two years of college. So we are actively looking. We are trying to buy more now."

Since investment comes from excess cash flow, I found that some families were hampered by the high cost of private schools. Many others found the funds for rental property investments. The young families were investing for their children's future college expenses, while those with a child already in college turned to investment property for financing all or part of the cost. Investing in property was a common practice within this group of upper-middle-class black families, and the majority were either invested or planning to invest.

Financial Wealth

The situation was different with financial investing. Fewer of these families owned stocks beyond those for retirement, and when they spoke of stock investments, there was less enthusiasm and more caution than when discussing investment properties. About a third of the couples affirmed that they owned stocks but often added a qualifier: "some stocks," a "small mutual fund," or "not a lot." Others noted that their stock ownership was only through their 401(k)s. Charlene Johnson, who spoke of stock options owned by both her and her husband, clarified their position by adding, "We're like 401(k) people. We just have this one little townhouse that we bought for investment, and we have that little IRA. And we have emergency funds." No one spoke of buying individual stocks or even mutual funds to pay for their children's college.

Although the Smiths, who owned investment properties, alluded to "deadbeat tenants," perhaps managing and profiting from investment properties is easier and even more lucrative than stocks for the small family investor. Stock market investing requires either a good deal of personal time and knowledge or the cost of a broker to manage these investments. Alfred Johnson, who also owned investment property, expressed this quandary when talking about stocks. "One, either you're on top of them, you have to monitor them daily, and time wise we don't have that. Secondly, if you pay somebody to do it, then you pay a lot in commissions. And then so you lose the real advantage." Robert Williams also addressed the time issue when speaking of their stock investments: "We have some mutual funds and stocks. I mean, we have stock in Sysco that I've had built over eight years, and although the market has kinda taken a big dive, you know, it's starting to change a little bit so that stuff has just been sitting. I haven't even really been paying attention to it. But we're not aggressive. Like, I definitely don't care to be in the stock market and be every day checking to see whether something is going up." His wife agreed, "We don't have time."

The Howards are an example of the active investors among this group. They were the couple who owned the house in North Carolina they rented to students. Frances Howard also emphasized that she contributed the max to her 401(k). The time problem, however, led to the end of an investment club they had participated in for ten years. She explained the problems the group faced in stock investing: "It was very useful. We learned a lot because the main philosophy in the investment group was that everybody would come with their investment opportunities or knowledge about a particular company or particular industry. And you know, you can pool small amounts of money, $100 each meeting. You can buy more with the group. But as time went on and people got busy with their kids' sports, and activities, we were meeting but we weren't really able to do the homework and bring that to the meeting. And we started having problems trying to find time to have the meetings. And so we kind of let it fall. We're hoping that maybe we can reactivate it."

The Matthews solved the time problem with the assistance of a niece who was a CPA. Like the Howards, they were seizing every opportunity for investing for their future.

LANDRY: You have a pension?
CYNTHIA: 401(k)s. We have a few investments and try to save.
LANDRY: This is property or stocks?
CYNTHIA: Stocks. And we try to do regular saving.
LANDRY: You have a broker, or you just pick it yourself? Mutual funds?
CYNTHIA: For me, we have two things through our jobs. Of course, you have to pick them yourself.

LANDRY: But apart from the job, do you have investments?

CYNTHIA: Yeah, we have a family fund with my sisters and nieces. We have a joint venture thing going.

HENRY: She's a CPA. Keeps track of where everything is going. Keeps us up-to-date.

CYNTHIA: We kind of have to read the stocks and, you know, make a decision.

HENRY: To buy new stocks.

Apart from the time issue, not everyone's experience in the market was as successful as that of the Matthews. Betty Thomas described her relationship with the stock market in the following way: "You know, I participate in my company's stock-purchase program. Used to be a little addicted to the stock market in the early 2000s but lost a little bit of money, and so I've been staying away from that. Brian participates more in that. But we have accounts at TD Waterhouse or TD Ameritrade now and Charles Schwab. I just leave my money in a little money market. I have a purchasing stock plan through Microsoft. They allow you to purchase company stock at a discounted rate. I do that every pay period."

Questions of time, knowledge, and risk arose in many of our conversations on the stock market. Michael Edwin represented the risk-averse position, that it was better to have investments that permit more "hands-on" control.

LANDRY: Do you think you can trust the market as a place to invest your money?

MICHAEL: I'm more apt to invest primarily in business. So, like, I have an investment company, a new company. I'm a start-up guy. So I like small companies. Ultimately I would love big equity stakes and a bunch of little companies that you help grow. To me, that's safer than the market 'cause I can have my hand in it. I mean, you don't have a hand in the market. There's nothing you can do. But there's something I can do primarily in business investment. I can extend my contacts, I can get more capital,

I can do whatever it is to help the probability of success. And that's how I'm oriented.

Retirement Funds

There is irony in the issues and obstacles voiced by these couples when discussing stock market investing. Preparing for retirement, except for Social Security, we are all "married to the bull," as one magazine headline shouted. Pensions, 401(k)s, and other retirement instruments are all invested in the stock market. Most employees can no longer take comfort in a guaranteed pension with a long-time employer, as in the past. Even some retirees with pensions are threatened with reductions. Not surprisingly, the most frequent retirement fund mentioned by these couples was the 401(k), which has replaced pensions in numerous companies. The couples I interviewed recognized the importance of this investment instrument for their future.

The most frequent statement I heard when talking about 401(k)s was this: "I do the maximum amount that they will match." Peggy Turner commented, "twenty-five. Why am I putting six grand [into my 401(k)]?" To which her husband replied, "This is the time you need to do it." Betty Thomas noted, "I participate in my 401(k). Always have since I understood the impact that it has."

At times, the discussion turned to the kind of retirement they expected to have. Denise Brooks, who believes she and her husband would be prepared to retire comfortably, said, "According to our financial advisor and the way we're planning, the way we're putting our money in, I think we will [be comfortable]. I don't think this is an extravagant lifestyle. We have a modest home, we're not going to Europe or the islands on a regular basis. Our vacations are local. We don't eat out a lot. So yeah, all the little trivial things that we're not big on. We're not buying BMWs. No. My next car will be a Toyota Corolla; I'm trying to go down. It just needs to move forward, that's all."

Patrick Harrington, who felt he had to delay his retirement because of his children's needs, was still optimistic. "Realistically, without the kids, I'd be done in three years. At fifty-five, I'd be finished. That's four years, I guess. But I got the kids now, so I got to extend that well beyond that time. So what are we gonna do? You know, we got a couple investments, we own some homes. And you know, I got a 401(k) and a little pension, a little Social Security, you know. It'll all add up. And it'll be fine. And we know that we won't require nearly as much for just the two of us. We won't require nearly as much as we require now. So we'll be fine. And then I don't think Judy's ever gonna stop; she's always gonna do some kind of work."

Not everyone was as optimistic about retirement. "As I get closer," Dennis Gilbert said, "I keep telling her [his wife] I'll have to keep working until I die." For John Berry, the question of retirement security drew a more complicated response.

> We both have 401(k)s. Now given everything we've just talked about—year off here, a year off there, trying to manage private school, we don't drive brand-new cars, our cars are paid for, but I've dipped into my 401(k), so I don't have as much as I used to. She's never touched hers, and you can see the difference. She probably has three-fold more in her account than what I've had in mine. I've worked for twenty years straight. I should probably have five-fold what I have, but I've had to dip into it for various things over the years. But we do have 401(k) plans. We have life insurance through our companies. We have all those things; but I don't feel completely secure, so there's some room for us to get better and to improve our standing there.

LANDRY: Do you contribute the max?
JOHN: I do, actually I do. I contribute the max. Given my salary, I contribute as much as I can.
LANDRY: So you are able to contribute the max, Kay?
KAY: I don't. I should, but I don't.

JOHN: I max out what the company matches, but again part of this thing is we have to keep our kids in private school, so that was part of it.

Overall, these couples seemed to be on track financially. Depending on employment in the private or public sector, they all had some kind of pension or 401(k), to which most contributed the maximum their employer matched. There were IRAs and other retirement plans and accounts. All of this was in addition to home equity, rental properties, stocks, and savings. Most families owned a mix of several retirement or investment accounts beyond the expected Social Security. Whether that would be enough for their retirement was still a question.

Earning a solid income and accumulating some wealth is the goal of most individuals and families. For this, they invest in the accumulation process from education to entry into the labor force. Yet the rate of success varies significantly between blacks and whites, even for those in the middle class. In spite of considerable improvement since 1964, middle-class blacks still lag behind their white counterparts, especially in wealth accumulation.

The thirty-one couples I interviewed went to college and secured careers. As their careers advanced and their families grew, they also increased their incomes and financial holdings. By all measures, they have been successful, in spite of obstacles faced. Securing the future of their children and their own retirement is the principal motivation for their wealth-accumulation efforts. In the next chapter, I focus on their attitudes and efforts on behalf of their children's education and future.

9
The Next Generation

The middle class grows in one of two ways, through the upward mobility of children of the working class or through the "inheritance" of their parents' class position by children of the middle class. When a daughter or son of middle-class parents remains in the middle class, sociologists use the term *inheritance*. It is not quite the same as parental genes reappearing as eye or hair color in their offspring. It represents middle-class parents' efforts in preparing their children to achieve this goal. Prominent among the resources used are the educational attainment of the parents and their economic means. The "race to the top" begins in preschool, some might even say in utero. Remember the Mozart craze? Although the usefulness of playing Mozart to a fetus in utero has been debunked, fetuses are subject to many influences. Nutrition of the mother affects not only physical but also mental development.

One might think that preparing children for the future is even more important for the African American middle class given the obstacles they face in the attainment process. Middle-class black parents have had their own experiences in school and in the workplace to guide them. The middle-class black families I interviewed in Prince George's County are no exception to this. Preparing their children for their future—a middle-class future—includes their educational goals for their children, their involvement in every phase of their education, and their financial sacrifices to ensure that they receive a quality education.

Educational Goals: "School Doesn't End Until You Graduate College"

Given the experiences of these parents in the workforce, they place great emphasis on their children attending college and earning, at least, a bachelor's degree. What surprised me somewhat was the vehemence with which they insisted that college was "not an option." They expressed this idea in many ways. For some, it came from their own experience growing up, regardless of the educational achievement of their parents. Tony Turner remembered his own experience growing up with college-educated parents. With his own background in mind, he spoke urgently about his educational aspirations for his son: "I want it to be like when I came up. I was probably in high school before I knew college was an option. My parents talked so much about college, their own. I didn't even know it was an option, believe it or not. I was a teenager and I was talking to somebody and asked, 'Where are you going to college?' and he was like, 'Shoot, I'm not gonna go to college.' I was like, 'You have to.' I thought it was just like regular school. I would get a list and I would pick where I wanted to go, but I had to go to a college. And my father said, 'Well, you do.' So I want my son to think the same, that college is never optional. I never remember a time of not knowing the concept of college."

Tony's wife, Peggy, whose parents were not college educated, recounted the same emphasis placed by her parents on gaining a college degree. "Education was everything to my mom because she never went to college. She said, 'You gotta get a good education. You gotta go to school [college].'" Some parents I interviewed emphasized the benefits of college as a preparation for life. More often, they spoke of the importance of a college degree for success in employment. Karen Gardner represented the first approach when she said, "But the main thing is just for them to go to college. Because I think you learn so much about yourself, about life. Just lessons that you can't get anywhere else other than in college. So they are definitely going to college. They even talk about college now, like where they're going to go." Kevin Tucker, who also placed a college education in a broader context, emphasized that a college degree was necessary "to be strong citizens and to help your community grow."

Troy Roberts, with a six-year-old daughter and a thirteen-year-old son, was very forceful in expressing the employment view.

LANDRY: What are your aspirations for your kids in terms of how far you want them to go?

TROY: They know college is after high school. You have to go to college and focus on a career that you want and then come out and still work hard to get the job that you want.

LANDRY: You're telling them that?

TROY: Yeah, I'm telling them. So they know, that this house wasn't just given to us. There's a mortgage you pay every month, and you pay a lot of money for this, a lot of money for that, schools cost money. So in order to do that, you got to have not a good job, but a good-paying job. There's a difference. You want to be happy at whatever you do, but you got to have the job that's going to provide what you want to do in life. And if you don't go to college, there's no other way you can get it.

The Andrews also represented the second position, stressing the changing educational requirements for success in the labor market. Richard emphasized, "I'd like for them to go as far as they can go. And we try to encourage them to get as much education [as possible]. It's so very important these days. When *we* came out of high school, you could come out of high school and get a job. You look at it now, it's very difficult." His wife, Barbara, supported his view, adding, "It's very competitive. So we're just encouraging them to just keep going to school as long as they possibly can."

The youngest and oldest couples were all of like mind in emphasizing the significance of a college degree and insisting it was not an option. Kevin Tucker was a thirty-five-year-old software engineer working on a master's degree in information technology (IT). His wife, Linda, also thirty-five, had an MA in bioscience and worked in organ transplant. With two children, six and eight years old, they did not hesitate to explain the importance they placed on a college degree.

KEVIN: We understand that education opens doors for you, and having your degree can open up a lot of doors and opportunities. And its tough out there, and it's getting tougher. You know, even in my type of field, which is more of an IT type of field, a lot of that work is being outsourced to other companies. So you have to be prepared, you have to be educated.

LINDA: You have to be educated. Honestly, I don't think it's going to be an option for them. I think, you know, the way we are raising them, they will look at college as that next step. And so [they'll say,] "When we graduate from the twelfth grade, then we go to college, Mommy." And so just instilling that in them early on and not saying it's an option for you not to go.

LANDRY: So they say that to you?

LINDA: Yes.

As the case of the Tuckers illustrates, these parents introduced the idea of college while their children were still very young. After speaking of the value of earning a master's degree, Jennifer Roberts continued, "I think we started instilling that in him [her thirteen-year-old son] since the third grade. When he could start writing and things like that. There are no choices [but to attend college]." The couples' children were absorbing these messages shaping their goals. "Andre [fourteen years old], he wants to do computer science," Shirley Edison said of her oldest son. "Victoria [twelve years old] wants to be a veterinarian." Of her three children, Barbara Andrew could say, "They think it [college] is not an option."

The Jamisons, whose two children had already graduated from college, explained how this happened.

LANDRY: So how did you prepare your children for college?

EDITH: You gotta go! And they always wanted to go to college.

MICHAEL: There's no [option]. As they grew up, we always talked about college. We enforced certain disciplines. And, you know, we put them around these people. We hung around people that were going in the same direction we wanted to go in.

MICHAEL: And they knew they were going.

Parental Involvement

Keeping college in the forefront proved to be a powerful strategy. Children responded willingly, even eagerly. Yet embracing the goal of a college education is only the first hurdle. The "sky is the limit" may be the mantra, but a great deal more is needed to reach this goal. As Karen Gardner expressed it, "I think now the emphasis needs to be not only to go to college but to finish college, to get a degree." Other parents, like the Smiths, stressed the need for academic preparation.

DOROTHY: I guess we're hoping that they are able to go to whatever school that they want to go. We want them to be able to go where they want to go by their test scores so that they shouldn't be denied any entrance anywhere, *anywhere* they want to go.

LANDRY: So college is understood?

DOROTHY: Oh yes, day one! Oh yeah, oh yeah! You come from some school; you wear the little sweatshirt with somebody's college on it. Oh yeah, oh yeah.

ARTHUR: At times we've had relatives who say, "Well, how do you know if they're gonna go? Maybe they won't want to go."

DOROTHY: No choice.

Parents understood that reaching the goal of a college degree required effort, preparation, and their involvement at every step. Involvement was the most frequent word I heard, involvement in their children's homework and involvement in their children's schools. Cynthia Matthews spoke of her involvement with the school and with her two children, who had already graduated from secondary school.

CYNTHIA: They did okay. I think that it's also part of how much parent participation your child has. I think kids do well if they know they have people behind them pushing them. If you just sort of send them and say do your work and leave them alone, they're gonna do just enough.

LANDRY: So what kinds of things did you do to keep them on track?

CYNTHIA: I'm at the school. I go to the school. I talk to and call the counselors. See what's going on.

LANDRY: You did that frequently?

CYNTHIA: Yeah. I want to see your schedule. Don't just sign up for a class. I want to see the schedule, and I call the counselor and say, "No, they're not taking that. They need to take an honor's class."

The Henrys, with a daughter majoring in electrical engineering at A&T University, were at pains to point out that her success was not just a result of her intelligence. Their involvement had played an important part.

SUE: When they come home from school, you're gonna check their homework, make sure they did their homework. You gonna be involved in the PTA. You know who the good teachers are.

ALFRED: You make them do a hundred extra problems. Yes.

LANDRY: Oh, you did that?

ALFRED: Yes. We used to make her do all the extra credit.

SUE: And they would come home with the odd numbers. He would say, "Do the even ones too."

ALFRED: Yeah, exactly.

With no sign of resentment, the daughter, who was present, added, "Read this book. Write a book report on all the books."

ALFRED: Yes, exactly. Read five extra books.

Some other parents were equally rigorous in monitoring their children's schoolwork. The following is Jerry Brooks's account of the couple's strategies.

JERRY: We do more, and our teacher said, "You all do more with him during homework time than most parents spend with their kids." So we have a set scheduled time for their homework, and every day there's some type of work they're doing. So you know we rarely give them a free day where they can just come home and relax, because they're doing reading math, or something like that.

LANDRY: And you're doing that with them?

JERRY: We're doing that with them. So we spend quality time with them. We check and make sure they're doing it right; we talk to the school teachers. When it's time to meet the teachers, or meet for PTA, we'll go to those kinds of things.

Alfred Henry, whose two children were in private schools, emphasized staying "vigilant" and not "taking a nap." They accomplished this in part by a "no TV deal during the week." Alfred explained: "So I would say, you know, we have some definite rules, and they're a little lax sometimes, but my heart is definitely in the right place. So we really have a no TV deal during the week. My last child, she might have watched a little bit of TV during the week, but we don't come in here and watch TV after school from five o'clock until nine thirty. That's never gonna happen. That's not even the culture, the environment that we've created here."

Some parents placed a premium on direct contact with the school personnel—principal and teachers. Kevin Tucker spoke with pride of his wife's involvement and that of parents in his neighborhood, in contrast with those at their previous location. The neighbors, he said, are "really involved with their kids, and that was really refreshing, coming out here and really seeing that. Parents really caring about going with their kids on the first day, meeting with the teachers, talking with the teachers. My wife is there all the time, the helper in the class, and things like that.

That's important for your children's development, and that makes the schools better because the teacher has more resources that they can pull from and anything that teacher needs, you have parents willing to go out there and buy it. If they need air-conditioning, they pool their money and then buy 'em an air conditioner."

Many parents recognized that involvement in a child's school brought access. Karen Gardner, who volunteered many hours in her child's school, related how on one occasion the principal kept another parent waiting while he talked to her. The incident strengthened her conviction of the benefit of involvement. "So it was like that parent was not important at all. That's why I'm telling you it makes a difference for your kid. It makes a big difference when the parent is involved and you let them know who you are, in terms of it being beneficial to your kid." "They give them the benefit of the doubt," added her husband. "And when there is an issue with our kid," Karen continued. "Because some things that happen to some parents they would not even consider that happening with us."

Kay Berry, who also had volunteered once a week in her daughter's school for an entire year, agreed with Karen. "That gave me leverage, you know. That allowed me to say, 'You know, I'm familiar with this teacher and I helped.' It's this extra little thing, and I'm hopeful that'll make a difference and get him in the class [she wanted]. It's all those little things. It's the access. It's what levers can you push."

As children get older, they are less inclined to acknowledge their parents' presence at school. Yet as an incident told by Karen confirms, children do want their parents' participation at school.

We have a program at our school called Hot Lunch, where the parents can come in because we don't have a cafeteria. So once a month they will have hot lunch, and parents can come in and have lunch with their kids. So we'd always go, and Mark would try to go when he could, but I would always go. And then I noticed our oldest son would just not acknowledge that I was there. And so, I'm thinking, "Wait a minute. Why am I wasting my time?" So then I don't go, and he's upset. "Why didn't you come?" "Because you don't acknowledge me when I'm there." And he says, "Well, I still expect you to come." And I'm like, "Well, could you at least say 'Hi' and that's it?" He's like, "Hi" and that's it, but I could tell he's looking to see if I'm there.

Enrichment and Exposure

Parents' involvement went beyond helping with homework, enforcing study rules, and volunteering in their children's schools. They spoke enthusiastically about enrichment activities and the necessity of exposing their children to "the wider world." Prominent among these enrichment activities were academic camps. Some began at a very young age, as Jennifer and Troy explained.

TROY: He did an enrichment camp this summer. His was tennis, piano, swimming, and chess. Not the everyday basketball camp, football. We gave him something totally different. And he just turned seven in June, and they had a chess tournament. He came in third.

JENNIFER: He had never played chess in his life and won third overall. He beat twelve- and thirteen-year-olds in chess.

LANDRY: Wow, that's impressive.

JENNIFER: Yeah, we were quite impressed. And the director of the camp was quite impressed with him. He's a quick learner.

Their thirteen-year-old son had also attended a summer health and science program at Howard University that required an application and a personal statement by the applicant. Jennifer explained, "So he was selected to participate in the program. He didn't have a fun summer, he was learning. For six weeks, he went to Howard University every day on campus. He went to classes, he had chemistry, science, math. They did make the enrichment program fun. Every Wednesday, they did some fun things, and every Friday took the kids on a field trip. So that afforded him an opportunity to walk across campus, see the university, how it kind of operates, the kind of students that go there, in classes, and the professors who came in and taught the seminars."

Some children went to nearby University of Maryland for academic day enrichment camps while others were sent away to residential camps. One of these was a "mock law program for kids," which the Whites' daughter attended in her sophomore year of high school. Of this program, Andrew White reflected, "I think to this day it is one of the best things that she had ever really been involved with. From what it seems, she enjoyed it. She learned a lot. Good exposure."

Alfred Henry spoke of the philosophy that motivated him in pursuing these activities for his daughter. "We need to uphold our part, keeping her focused and then enriching her. If there're some things that the public school can't do for her, then that's where we come in and spend extra dough doing enrichment things during the summer." In addition to a summer soccer camp at the University of Maryland, he continued, "she's been away to their program for talented and gifted students in Washington County, called the Washington Summer Centers. She went to that two different years. One year she was in a Writing Strand program. That was a residency overnight weeklong program. There was a screening process. Six-page application to get there, and you had to be recommended and selected. So we've had her into a lot of different activities. She gets along with everybody. She's always looking forward to new opportunities."

Beyond academic enrichment, parents spoke of "exposure." As Thomas Edison put it, "The external exposure is what we're trying to give him. Everything from horseback riding to playing tiddly-winks, to going up to the skate park." He stressed, "I mean it's exposing him to all—to the world. . . . He's scuba diving. We let him go down fifty feet; you're on your own, go out. And it's the exposure to all the other things. It's kind of like balance. Yes, there's the academic, yes we're going to drive you, this is what you need to do, and you know, this is the expectation, but it's not necessarily [everything]."

Christine and Steve Edwards commented on how they exposed their two children, seven and eleven years old.

CHRISTINE: We travel a lot with them. We expose them to a lot.

STEVE: We took them to California, went to see the Hoover Dam, Valley of Fire, which is some mountains.

CHRISTINE: It's just like the Grand Canyon; it's a smaller version of the Grand Canyon.

STEVE: Outside of Vegas. It's really beautiful. Really, it's kind of like life changing if you go out there and just see it. It's beautiful.

Exposure often included many lessons: musical instruments, sports, and art.

CHRISTINE: They take piano lessons, ballet lessons. Just exposing them to as much as we can. When it comes to their lessons, making sure that they practice and they do the best that they can.

STEVE: You want them to see beyond their immediate surroundings so they know that there is a lot more out there for them.

CHRISTINE: And we also try to get them involved in political things. Like we took them to a rally: "Save the environment." I try to expose them to things that are happening in the world because now the world is more global.

Jerry and Denise Brooks also saw traveling as "a part of their [children's] education."

JERRY: We save for when we want to take them on a vacation during spring break.

DENISE: And that's a part of their education as well. It's not just fun for us. He's been to Disneyworld and museums. So we're trying to build in the Montessori approach throughout our vacations and our lives because we think it works for children.

Many enrichment and exposure activities accompanied the already extensive and time-consuming efforts to support schoolwork.

While sometimes tiring, these parents were dedicated and focused on preparing their children for college and for life beyond.

Choosing a School: Public or Private

The poor performance of the Prince George's County public school system complicated parents' goal of preparing their children for college. As discussed in chapter 5, this was in part the outcome of the school system's history, the turmoil accompanying efforts to desegregate the schools through court-ordered busing, and a lack of funds. Parents faced the dilemma of choosing between public and private schools. Private schools had the advantage of smaller classes and forced parental participation, but the disadvantage of high tuitions. The difference in a teacher-pupil ratio of 1:30 in public schools compared to 1:16 in private schools was considered a decided advantage by many parents who complained of over-crowding in public schools. Speaking about classroom size, Tony Turner summarized his views in the following way: "I think that's probably why we see more parochial schools, church schools in the area, because they are compensating for the overcrowding. Not that I think the schools closest to us are bad schools as far as academics. Their primary issue is overcrowding, and that's the key problem that the teacher ratio is 1:30. That's too much. And that's what's suffering. It's not that the teachers are not trained or the teacher's not educated. It's a shortage."

Parental involvement was universally touted as a necessary ingredient for success. This appeared to give private schools an edge, according to Troy Roberts. "The difference between the private school and the public schools: the public school doesn't force the parents to be involved. And the private school forces you because, one, you're paying the money; two, they're always communicating with you. If you're in that large classroom size, the child can get left behind. And they may not get what they need to go to the next grade."

The Gardners spoke approvingly of the volunteer requirement of private schools. Karen noted, "Each family is required to have thirty volunteer hours. You have to volunteer thirty hours of your time, every year. But last year Morris and I had 160 hours."

The cost of a private school education was not trivial, however, and kept some children in public schools. Troy Roberts, who spoke so enthusiastically of the private school's communication with parents, still felt the pinch of the tuition cost. "Both of my kids have been in private school since they've been in kindergarten. I am tired of paying. My son is going into high school, and we are considering sending him to public high school because we have this new superintendent who is trying to make effective changes now."

James Douglas put a figure on the cost of private schools for his two children. "I figure we spent, from third to twelfth, we spent $100,000 in education fees." Kay Berry, with two children in private schools, spoke of a tuition bill of $18,000 a year. Her husband, John, raised the figure to $20,000 because of the added cost of after-school lunch. Kay added, "Nine thousand a kid, which as private schools go isn't all that exorbitant. But golly, it sure does feel like it when you're doing that check every month."

Some of the most satisfied parents were those whose children tested into the talented and gifted program (TAG) or entered a magnet school or program through the lottery. They believed that their children would receive an education equal to private schools without the cost of tuition. Linda and Kevin Tucker, a happy couple whose two young children, six and eight years old, won the lottery for the Montessori magnet program, rejoiced at their good fortune. "So they were there [in a private Montessori school since two years old], and we were blessed enough to be able to get picked in the lottery for the magnet school, so we could take them out of the private school." "And didn't have to pay that mortgage," Kevin added. "Yeah, that was a mortgage," she continued. "That was almost equal to our mortgage at the townhouse."

Parental Assessment of the Public Schools

There were different assessments of the public school system. Some parents strongly defended it and decried the lack of parental involvement, which they argued undermined the system with a "drop-off mentality." The Hamiltons were committed to the public schools, as long as their two children, six and eight years, could receive a quality education. Brad explained his approach: "Yeah, I mean, let's be honest. I'm not a fool, I value education. If they didn't get into a magnet school, I'd probably have to send them to a private school as well. Because you don't want to sacrifice your child's education and future for your own personal rants that I just went on." Others saw the public school system as a failure and bore the costs of private tuition, a sometimes agonizing decision, as Kay Berry admitted. "People struggle with this because this was the pillar of the civil rights movement. This is something we feel strongly about." Still others used both public and private schools, moving from one to the other depending on grade level, child's performance, or costs. A family might have children in both public and private schools. Perhaps Troy Roberts, who expressed frustration over the cost of private schools, summed up best the position of involved parents: "No matter where they go, we'll still be doing homework together. We'll still be studying, working together, doing things because that's some of the downfalls you have in public schools. The parents aren't involved."

College

A few families had children in college or recently graduated from college. The majority still faced the daunting tasks associated with entrance into college: selection, visiting, writing essays, and financing. These tasks are the proximate activities required for entry into college. Parents also knew that preparation for college began much earlier: in the selection of elementary and high schools and in the academic achievement of their children during these early years. Summer academic programs were often cited as part of college preparation. My question about college preparation received this answer from Linda Tucker, who had two children, six and eight years old: "We're always trying to put them into something where they're going to learn more and to expose them to different careers. For example, this summer, our son was in an NSBE program—National Society of Black Engineers. They had a pilot program this summer for children third grade to fifth grade, their NSBE junior program. And in this program, the children build everything. They show that they can engineer things and make them work. So it was a three-week program." Frank Harrison, whose son was twelve, followed a similar strategy. The father explained, "He is in an academic enrichment summer camp now at Queen Anne's, where he's taking math because he is kinda slow in math."

The selection of a high school was especially important because of its proximity to college, as Charles Brody noted.

LANDRY: Have you all started thinking about preparation for college?

CHARLES: Yes, I think that's part of why we're picking the schools that we are. Because, you know, we're thinking about schools that are strong academically but they also have a number of extracurriculars. I would call them extended learning opportunities that are there that foster a certain amount of independence, a certain amount of critical thinking. There are also outside activities that we get the children involved with, to help them to be independent, to be responsible.

Other parents, like the Hamiltons, spoke of exposing their children to the college environment itself as preparation.

LANDRY: So what kinds of things have you done to prepare them for college?

BRAD: We teach them about college. As Debbie pointed out, we try to take them to A&T and expose them to the college experience a little bit.

DEBBIE: We expose them to the University of Maryland, they go to Maryland Day, other things, just to see, you know, what a college is like.

James and Mary Douglas, whose son was in a prefreshman program at Morehouse College, was an example of the multiple things parents did to prepare their children for college. James noted: "We spend a lot of money. I mean the summer program at Delaware State, Howard. We did the Kaplan thing. We went to Sylvan. We had an SAT tutor come to the house and work with him with the SAT." All parents were familiar with the importance of AP classes as well as the PSAT and SAT. Children in high school had already taken these tests or were planning to do so.

CHOOSING A COLLEGE

African American parents face a unique issue in their children's college choice: historically black colleges or universities (HBCUs) or predominantly white colleges? Some parents felt that their children needed to solidify their black identity before pursuing a postgraduate degree or entering the labor force. For these parents, an HBCU was the place for their children to earn a college degree. This was the choice of James and Mary Douglas, whose seventeen-year-old son was in a prefreshman program at Morehouse College, an HBCU. His father explained.

JAMES: I wanted him to get that experience because I thought he's moving away from that.
LANDRY: In what way?
JAMES: The friends he hangs around with were all white. Not that that's a bad thing. But he needed survival skills as a black man. I thought he would get it better there. He would get the nurturing. He'd get it at an HBCU.

The Andrews felt the same way. Richard explained that they had chosen Morehouse for their son because of "the leadership that they instill in the black men there." He continued with a sentiment shared by his wife: "I think that it would be good for him to be in an environment that he's familiar with and also be supported. And I'm not sure just how much support he would get in a predominantly white school, you know. Not that that might not be a choice if the time comes. But I really feel that he would have an opportunity to be strengthened in that [HBCU] environment. Now, maybe for your master's program, you kinda have a good feel of what you're dealing with. So you'd be much more mature and be able to handle that environment."

Frances and Joseph Howard had raised their two daughters to anticipate going to an HBCU. "We raised them knowing where they were going to go. From infancy." They also saw graduate school at a white school as a choice coming after formation in an HBCU. "She can go to those schools [mostly white] when she gets her graduate degree."

Brenda White spoke more openly about differences in the environments of HBCUs and mainly white colleges and about what she thought would be better for her daughter. "The balance is, I know culturally she will get a better education from an HBCU because there will be other factors that she won't have to deal with. She won't have to deal with being in the classroom and being the only black and people automatically assuming that you're not qualified. They don't want to be your lab partner because they don't want to do all the work because you don't know anything. You don't have to deal with that when you're in black schools, but when you're in a white school it's right there in your face. And that's a different type of stressor."

Some parents took a pragmatic position depending on the particular needs of each child. Judy Harrington, who had persuaded one daughter to attend an HBCU, noted, "I thought, it was the right choice [for one daughter]. Because each child is different and you want your kids to go to school and get a degree. That's one thing you want. My other daughter, she can go wherever, and you know she can't be torn down. But that one, she could be. And I needed to protect her a little more. And to me HBCUs make you feel like when you leave there you can conquer the world, and other schools make you doubt yourself. And I've gone to both, and I've experienced both. And I learned how to put it all together. Now she's gonna go to graduate school. And she'll be able to go to whatever graduate school she wants to go to."

Not all parents gave priority to HBCUs. Some expressed indifference to the choice between an HBCU and a white college or were undecided. Other families were divided in their preferences. Sometimes, one child went to an HBCU while another chose a white college. Linda Tucker fell in the first category. She explained, "You know what, it doesn't make a difference to me. It really doesn't, as long as they're getting the education they need. As long as they're getting a good education, it really doesn't make a difference. I mean, I'm not one to say, 'Okay, it has to be black.' As you see, we like diversity, and you know, being diverse helps you to be a better person and to understand the world better." Kevin echoed his wife's sentiment: "It doesn't matter for me." Margaret Francis gave the same response to my question about type of school. "You know I really don't care. I just want them to be happy and enjoy it."

The Edisons' two oldest children, fourteen and twelve, seemed to be heading to different colleges. "I already talked to Victoria about going to an HBCU," Shirley explained. "Andre, I'm not sure. He wanted to go to Virginia Tech." Other parents spoke of finding a good "fit" for their children or stressed wanting them to "be happy" wherever they went. This was the case of the Berrys, with three children, five, nine, and thirteen. As Kay expressed it, "I want them to get into the best school, but I also want it to be the best fit and I want them to be happy and all of that."

Jerry Brooks, whose youngest child was only seven, expressed the dilemma that many African American families feel in the choice of a college for their children. "Warren's seven. He's in the third grade; nine more years of school. Wherever we want to send them to school, our biggest thing right now is do we want to send our kids to an HBCU? Or if Warren or Page get selected to go to Harvard or a Yale, what do we do? And that's our biggest issue right there for us. Do we send them to Morehouse or Spellman, or do we send them to Yale or Tuskegee? So we have to rationalize that in our minds because we don't want the HBCUs to die."

Beyond the quandary that some parents felt between an HBCU and a largely white college, there was also their children's preferences. One of the Gilberts' daughters wanted to attend Brown University and did so. "She really wanted to go to Brown," her mother said. "But then we decided to find some middle schools that she would look at. So she was accepted at Georgetown and at Washington University. But she really wanted to go to Brown."

One of Henry and Cynthia's sons "was really adamant about staying close to home" and went to Howard University in the District. In the end, it was a compromise.

CYNTHIA: We tried to get him to go to North Carolina or just kind of venture out. He's very adamant about it.

HENRY: "I'm not going."

CYNTHIA: We didn't push it because he was really adamant about staying close to home.

HENRY: But he's gonna stay on campus.

CYNTHIA: He's staying on campus. Yes. That was our requirement. If you stay close to home you need to be on campus.

HENRY: College life—you really need to be on campus to really experience it.

CYNTHIA: And to grow. Just to kind of grow and become independent as his own person, which is hard to do when living with your parents.

Although, as we saw earlier, some parents were insistent on their children attending an HBCU, many played an influential role in the decision without determining the outcome. "I want them to go to a school that is diverse," Karen Gardner admitted. "But I would support the decision for wherever they want to go to college." The oldest Edwards child wanted to attend a California college. Steve was accommodating in his decision: "It's up to them."

Financing is an integral part of choosing a college. What can a family afford? How will tuition be covered? Are scholarships available? How much must be borrowed? For some parents, the cost of college tuition was an expense besides the recent financing of private elementary and/or high school. The trillion dollars in outstanding student loans today speaks loudly about the high cost of tuition, even at public colleges and universities. With the decline in state support of public colleges from 32 percent in 2003 to only 23 percent in 2012, according to a GAO study, tuition has taken a significant hit, rising from 17 to 25 percent during the same period. Public colleges and universities are no longer inexpensive alternatives to private colleges. Financing a child's college education grows ever more challenging. Yet parents know that without a college education, the middle class would be virtually out of reach for their children. For this reason, they are willing to make large economic sacrifices to finance their children's college education.

Financing a college education for one child can be difficult enough. Most families have two or three children. Among the thirty-one families I interviewed, five had one or more children who had already completed college, and four others had one or two children in college. The rest were planning for the future.

Claudia and Dennis Gilbert's financing of their two daughters' college education was complicated.

DENNIS: The oldest one, what did we do? We paid for the first year for Judy. We paid the first year.

CLAUDIA: Didn't she get some money?

DENNIS: The third and fourth year, but I think the first year we paid. And she got a partial scholarship, that first year and the second year, but we primarily got loans for Judy. . . . And then Charlene?

CLAUDIA: Brown gave her half tuition.

The Gilberts encountered a catch-22. When they found another scholarship, Brown University reduced proportionally what they were offering. Claudia reflected on their dilemma. "And any other scholarship she got, they ate that. Oh God, yeah. So we stopped looking."

Financial arrangements for meeting college expenses varied greatly. The Bells fared better than the Gilberts since one son received tuition remission because his mother worked at the school. Their younger son "took out his own loans," while his parents paid the tuition at the University of Maryland. Both children of Edith and Michael Jamison were fortunate to have graduated with no loans. Their son received a full athletic scholarship, and they paid for their daughter's college in full.

MICHAEL: We didn't pay the mortgage sometimes, but her tuition got paid. We decided enough people struggled with loans after the fact, after graduation, and we didn't want to be a part of that. So we paid every single cent.

EDITH: Part of our budget.

MICHAEL: Part of our budget. We paid it. It hurt.

LANDRY: How were you able to save for that?

MICHAEL: No, we didn't. See, we didn't have big savings. It was cash and carry.

EDITH: That's how we did it. School was just in our budget anyway.

For those families with children in college, I heard equally diverse stories. James Douglas, whose son, as we saw above, was in a prefreshmen program at Morehouse, explained the twists and turns that occurred in their case.

JAMES: I started out trying to save on my own. And I realized that I had too many emergencies. So I kept dipping into it. I said, "This is not going to work." So when he was in the seventh grade, the Maryland Legislature passed the Tuition—

MARY: Prepaid tuition [529 college savings plan].

JAMES: Prepaid tuition plan, and so I got into that when he was in his seventh grade and paid my contract up by the time he was in the tenth grade, fully expecting him to go to a Maryland school.

And now he's going out of state, so you know. The Maryland 529 will still pay the way [in an out-of-state college] as an average of the tuitions of the state of Maryland, so I still get that part, but the rest of it I'm paying out of pocket.

Another pattern that emerged was a child receiving a partial or full scholarship in the first year only. This was the case of the Howards, the Matthewses, and the Henrys. Families solved the problem of financing for the full four years in different ways. The Howards's oldest daughter received a variety of "community scholarships" that paid for 60 to 70 percent of her first-year expenses. "But this year I think we'll be paying more," her mother commented. "'Cause those were like the first year. Those weren't four years. So she's applying for some other scholarships, small $2,000 here, $2,500 here. Those kinds of things. She hasn't heard back from them yet." Cynthia Matthews had a similar experience with her son, who was in his first year of college. "Well, he got a scholarship, piece of scholarship. And we'll probably do some loans I'm sure." In response to my question on saving for college, her husband, Henry, replied with both regret and optimism. "You know, that's one of the regrets that I do have, not putting aside like we should have. So that wouldn't hurt as much. But it's gonna work out, and everything is gonna be fine. He won't have any problems. He won't feel a thing."

Sue and Alfred Henry financed their eldest daughter's college with "some scholarship from the school" for the first year, with the rest to be financed by loans and out of pocket. There were still two younger daughters whose college expenses had to be financed. Discussing this challenge, Alfred said, "We'll have to make some adjustments. Bottom line is we'll do what we have to do. But something tells me, I'll just say this, I think in my mind, I'm getting prepared to pay because if you're talking about what I know, I'm dreaming about, there aren't many scholarships to Columbia or Princeton or Harvard."

Some parents with young children did not yet have a plan in place for financing college. Yet, as Kevin Tucker explained, he and his wife were already thinking about college costs for their two children, six and eight years old. "We're looking at 529-type programs for them in college, bonds, and things like that. But we haven't put away serious amounts of money for their education. The plan is that we will put money away because it sort of costs a lot if they don't get scholarships or some sort of help." Some others were very early planners. The Turners, with a three-year-old son, already had a 529 plan that Peggy emphasized was started "the year he was born." They explained their goals for their son.

TONY: All the money that I get from my side job, my teaching [is saved for college]. I do project management instruction.

PEGGY: Our goal is to put [away] at least $15,000 a year; that's our goal.

TONY: My goal is that wherever he says he wants to go, I won't have to say no because of money. That's my goal.

Having earned bachelor's and even advanced degrees, having developed successful careers, sometimes against formidable obstacles, the middle-class blacks I interviewed took the next step: promoting the achievement of their children. They placed their cultural, social, and economic capital at the disposal of their children's educational and personal growth, with the goal of smoothing their paths into the middle class. There seemed to be no sacrifice too great for these parents, whose experience reminded them that the stakes are high. The generations represented by these thirty-one couples traversed several economic and cultural periods and ushered in another generation that will continue the growth of the African American middle class. The lessons they learned are passed on to their children's generation as they follow in the footsteps of their parents. Next, in the Afterword, I discuss changes in the lives of middle-class blacks in the Prince George's County suburbs since 2007.

Afterword

2007 to the Present

Since 2007, there have been significant changes in Prince George's County in the areas of politics, education, and services. I begin with politics, the area that has captured the most public attention. Wayne K. Curry was Prince George's County's first black county executive; he followed Parris N. Glendening, who served three terms from 1982 to 1994. Unlike Glendening, Curry served for only two terms (1994–2002) because the county had voted in a two-term limit for the county executive and County Council members in 1992. Jack B. Johnson followed Wayne Curry and also served for two terms (2002–2010).

During Johnson's tenure as county executive, there arose the rumor that business in Prince George's County was operating under a "pay to play" system. Johnson was indicted on November 12, 2010, for kickbacks and taking bribes in his last year, charges for which he finally pleaded guilty and was convicted and sentenced to prison for over seven years. Johnson's wife, Leslie, was also convicted and was sent to prison for one year and a day. The charges and convictions caused much consternation in the county, which was already very sensitive about its image. Many residents felt hurt and betrayed.

Rushern L. Baker III succeeded Johnson as county executive in 2010. Baker had earlier served in the Maryland House of

Delegates from 1994 to 2003, a position from which he garnered political experience and a broad view of the county's issues. Upon confirmation, Baker faced the continuing problems of the Prince George's school system. His first challenge came with the unexpected resignation of school superintendent William Hite in 2012, who left to assume the position of school superintendent in Philadelphia. Hite had served as interim school superintendent following the departure of John Deasy in 2009 after just two years as superintendent, and was then elected school superintendent later that year. Both Hite, who is white, and Deasy, who is black, were credited with significant improvements in student achievement. Nevertheless, Hite was one of four school superintendents since 1999, and the only one to serve for four years. In 2012, the county once again faced the challenge of finding another leader of a school system with 125,000 students and a $1.6 billion budget at a time of both financial and academic challenges. An increasingly frustrated legislature threatened a takeover of the school system.

Baker sought a solution by following the paths of New York City and Washington, D.C., where Mayors Michael Bloomberg and Adrian Fenty had each gained control of their troubled school systems. In Prince George's County, the school board and the teachers' union bitterly opposed the idea. The Maryland legislature approved a hybrid plan. Baker was given the authority to appoint the school superintendent and several of the school board members. The school board was tasked with improving student achievement and maintained control of the budget. Nevertheless, this new arrangement reduced the school board's power and enhanced that of the superintendent. Despite the rancor surrounding restructuring, the public school system's administration and the school board moved forward, with Baker receiving considerable support from the new school board.

After running unopposed and being reelected in 2014, Baker again faced challenges in his second term. The recession of 2008 led to a fiscal crisis in Maryland, and funding for Prince George's school system decreased, as I noted in chapter 5. In the same year as Baker's reelection, a state audit severely criticized the school system for many flaws, including weak financial controls and oversight of expenditures. To make up for the revenue shortfall, Baker proposed a 2016 budget that would include a 15 percent increase in property tax over three years. The increased tax would bring in an additional $135.7 million for the school system. This was a bold move that Baker argued was needed to raise the level of student achievement to be on par with other county school systems. Stakeholders lined up on both sides of the proposal. On one side was the opposition of longtime residents, many of whom had helped pass TRIM (Tax Reform Initiative by Marylanders) in 1978, a law that froze property taxes. Some civic associations and police and fire unions joined the opposition. Newer residents, the teacher's union and administrators, CASA [an important Latino nonprofit], and the Prince George's Business Roundtable lined up to support Baker's plan. Some in opposition wondered how the money would translate into higher academic performance or fretted about a property tax already high compared to neighboring counties. Others saw potentially huge benefits that a competitive educational system could bring to the county.

Despite TRIM, which the residents of Prince George's County had overwhelmingly upheld against a challenge in 1996, Baker based his argument for a tax increase on a 2012 law that sanctioned a property tax increase above TRIM if the revenue raised went to public education. While accepting the 2012 law, the County Council refused to support Baker's proposal for a 15 percent property tax increase, opting instead for a 4 percent increase. In part, the action reflected their perception of the voters' opposition to a 15 percent increase and irritation over Baker's failure to consult and negotiate with them on his tax proposal. Baker vetoed parts of the budget passed by the County Council and urged passage of a compromise 11.45 percent increase, but to no avail as the council unanimously overrode his budget veto. In the end, the County Council passed the first property tax increase since TRIM, but the $34 million in new tax revenues for the school system was not enough for Baker and the school superintendent's major proposals.

Nevertheless, both Baker and council members pledged to work together for the good of the school system and county. Several important issues were still in the hopper, including efforts to attract a proposed new FBI headquarters to the county. Analysts noted that the "budget war" was an exception to the smooth working relationship and support that Baker enjoyed with the County Council in his first four-and-one-half years as county executive.

Services

As we saw in chapter 5, the most frequent complaint, after school quality, of Prince George's County middle-class residents was the lack of upscale dining and shopping. This changed in 2010 when Wegmans supermarket opened. For many, Wegmans' entrance in Prince George's County was especially sweet since Prince George's had won over its wealthier neighbor, Montgomery County. This was a big coup because Wegmans, called the "holy grail" of grocers by one reporter, is extremely careful in selecting locations for its stores and only opens two or three a year nationwide.[1] It is a large gourmet supermarket with many amenities such as a sushi chef, a wine bar, a restaurant, and live music. Residents considered this a vindication of their market power and a signal to other merchants that had heretofore avoided settling in the county. Since its opening, Wegmans has also gained the reputation of a social hot spot, attractive to singles and groups. More than any other supermarket chain, Wegmans exemplifies the changes roiling the industry at a time when a supermarket, like a bookstore, is perceived as more than just a place to shop. Bookstores long ago added cafés with an array of coffee choices, Wi-Fi, pastries, and sandwiches to attract customers. Now supermarkets recognize that many customers want more, and Wegmans seems ahead of the curve in accommodating them. Karen Thomas, a spokeswoman for the Food Marketing Institute trade group, said that supermarkets "have to meet customers' needs and have what customers want. Some stores hold cooking classes and offer children's programs."[2] Wegmans' amenities were described in a *Washington Post* article several months after its opening. "Wi-Fi encourages people to linger with their laptops. Flat-panel televisions lure locals to watch the news or a basketball game. Fireplaces and comfortable chairs invite book clubs to meet. Restaurants offer gourmet meals."[3]

Wegmans, located in the Woodmore Towne Centre, is one of four anchor stores. This is a 245-acre mixed-use development that will include office space, hotels, and residential units. Most recently, the county administration attracted Nordstrom Rack, an off-price retail division of Nordstrom, Inc., to open in 2016 in the same development. This is an improvement over retail venues available in the past. Yet a full Nordstrom still eludes the county.

Perhaps because of Wegmans' location in Prince George's County, Whole Foods finally opened a new store in the county in 2017, capping efforts by the county over six years to attract more upscale services. Despite not having the elevated reputation of Wegmans, Whole Foods is a highly sought after supermarket for its perceived quality and offerings, considerable selection of organic produce, deli, bakery, and extensive array of prepared hot and cold food. Additionally, what some call the "Whole Foods effect" is expected to become an "engine for development" in the area, attracting other businesses, housing, and residents.[4] Its role as the anchor in the Riverdale Park multiuse $250 million development suggests that the service drought in the county may be coming to an end.

National Harbor

I discussed Wegmans and Whole Foods before National Harbor, established in 2008, because these two supermarkets were for county residents. National Harbor is a development for the region and the nation. This three-hundred-acre multiuse development on the Potomac River in Prince George's County boasts of a convention center, thirty dining venues, 150 stores, Tanger Outlets, a farmers' market, and recreational opportunities that include a 180-foot-high Ferris wheel called the Capital Wheel. Given its waterfront location, there are also water taxis and one of the best marinas in the region.

National Harbor was not built primarily for the residents of Prince George's County. Its name, and the widespread use of "national" in the titles of a large variety of venues, underscores this. Still, National Harbor is *in* Prince George's County and is accessible to its residents. There are national-brand hotels but none that reach the four-star level. Among the many restaurants, only four are ranked above four stars, and the highest is 4.5 stars. However, five-star restaurants are a rarity, with Washington, D.C., claiming only one 4.9-star restaurant with the next highest ranked 4.7. Neighboring Montgomery County, known for its rich gastronomy in Bethesda, has only two restaurants with a 4.6 ranking. Although not built for Prince George's County specifically, National Harbor's location in the county has brought much-needed restaurants and shops only twenty miles from Mitchellville. More recently, a $1.4 billion MGM Casino opened in National Harbor after a long debate over its merits for the county. Again, although there are benefits for the county in terms of employment and financial receipts, the casino was built for the metropolitan area and not for Prince George's County specifically.

The 2008 Economic Downturn

The housing crisis and recession beginning in 2007 were not kind to the residents of Prince George's County. While foreclosures and underwater mortgages were widespread nationally and in the Washington, D.C., metro area, Prince George's County suffered more than other counties. In 2010, 4.6 percent of housing loans were in foreclosure in Prince George's County, twice the metropolitan rate of 2.3 percent. Mortgage delinquency of ninety days or more was 9.3 percent compared to 4.2 percent in the metropolitan area. If a recent study that attributes a significant portion of the black-white wealth gap to inequity in housing value is correct, then the housing crisis may well have reduced the housing wealth of many Prince George's residents and widened the wealth gap, even for those in the upper middle class. Still, a 2010 study by the Maryland National Park and Planning Commission found that the highest foreclosure risks were in sections of the county other than the middle-class areas.[5] Three major consequences of the housing crisis affect homeowners: lowered housing values and equity, underwater mortgages, and foreclosures. One or more of these three consequences were felt by probably the majority of homeowners regionally and nationally. To understand fully and accurately how Prince George's black middle class fared during this period, we need to parse out these three effects. Summary statistics for the whole county or even for one or two neighborhoods can be misleading.

Although all residents experienced a loss of housing market value and equity, losses varied directly with the purchase date of a home. In my study, I found that most of the thirty-one couples had realized at least a two- to three-fold increase in their home market value and equity by 2007. All but a few had bought their final home in the 1980s or 1990s, a period of rising housing values. Those who bought their homes after 2000 had less opportunity for a significant rise in their market values and equity. These homeowners suffered the most.

A study by the *Washington Post* of the effects of the housing crisis in Prince George's County focused on Fairwood, a community with eighteen hundred residents.[6] To understand the crisis that engulfed Fairwood, it is necessary to know that this community of 73 percent black homeowners with a medium income of $170,000 opened in 2005, shortly before the housing market tanked. Those who bought homes in Fairwood after 2005 were paying the high prices generated by housing market growth in the 1980s and 1990s. They did not have the same opportunity for growth in market value and equity as the earlier buyers I interviewed. When the housing market plummeted, they were prime candidates for underwater mortgages and foreclosure. Adding to their vulnerability was the high percentage who had subprime mortgages, 28 percent of the 1,441 homes bought between 2006 and 2007, according to the *Washington Post*'s study. Even more shocking, the same article reports that in the years immediately before the crisis, 31 percent of middle-class blacks with incomes over $200,000 received subprime mortgage loans. Fairwood suffered one of the highest rates of foreclosure in the county. Many homeowners had underwater mortgages. To some extent, it was timing. Middle-class blacks who bought much earlier lost market value and equity but not their homes. It was different with those purchasing homes after 2005. Other studies have found that black home buyers of all classes were disproportionately targeted by lenders—including some of the largest banks—for subprime loans.

The experience of middle-class blacks in Prince George's County during and after the housing crisis and recession that followed is a cautionary tale with many facets. Because Prince George's County is predominantly black, because it lacks the services of neighboring predominantly white counties, and because of its underperforming school system, it is not a magnet for homebuyers and businesses like the other nearby counties, nor is it an area of ever increasing market value that a racially diverse county creates. While a number of circumstances created an unusual opportunity for developing the wealthiest upper-middle-class black suburban community in the country, it had an Achilles' heel. If Prince George's County had the services and quality of schools of some of its neighbors, its story might have evolved differently during this period. The recovery of its housing market and precrisis accumulated wealth is lagging behind those of neighboring majority-white counties.

The county remains an important example of black middle-class suburbanization and wealth accumulation. Yet the national housing crisis and recession revealed the vulnerabilities of black suburban communities during rapid demographic and economic change. The African American Dream still has many hurdles in both good times and bad times.

Conclusion

The Twenty-First Century

Writing about African American life is difficult. Always it is a story of life half full or half empty. I try to find a balance while recognizing that some readers will interpret the findings as more positive or more negative than warranted by the data. This is still the dilemma of African American life—including that of the upper middle class—in the twenty-first century. So after nine chapters, what can we conclude about the new black middle class in the twenty-first century? In many ways, I would say it is as far from its emergence in the late 1960s as computers are from the typewriters of that time. Yet there are areas where the black middle class seems to be stuck in the twilight zone of racial discrimination. In chapter 6, I introduced the concept of attainment, which sociologists use to analyze and measure upward mobility. This concept can be used to compare black middle-class achievement in the twenty-first century with that of the past. In 1968, sociologist Otis Dudley Duncan published an article on mobility with the title "Inheritance of Poverty or Inheritance of Race?"[1] Using a national representative sample of black and white males age twenty-five to sixty-four with nonfarm backgrounds,[2] he addressed the burning issue of that period: the causes of poverty and the higher rate of poverty among blacks compared to whites. Unlike many other researchers at the time, Duncan concluded that race was a major cause of intergenerational poverty. He wrote, "Handicaps have effects in producing Negro-white differences at each stage of the life cycle. Handicaps at one stage are transmitted to subsequent stages and reflected in differences there as well. In addition, at each stage, there are further substantial gaps not explained by the accumulation of prior handicaps but specific to the way the structure works at the stage itself."[3]

His argument is that all the disadvantages (handicaps) suffered by blacks, compared to whites, at one point in time (e.g., a generation) are carried forward and negatively impact the achievement of the next generation. Low educational and occupational attainment in one generation impacts the educational, occupational, and income attainment of the next generation. In introducing the term "structure," he emphasized that societal institutions (what some have called "institutional racism") add a handicap over and above handicaps coming from the past. He concluded that poverty was not caused by an inheritance of poverty but by the handicaps that blacks encountered at each stage of the life cycle because of their race. In his own words: "Inheritance of poverty is of lesser consequence in the whole picture of such gaps than the aggregate of all the forms of discrimination."[4]

Duncan noted that this also applied to middle-class blacks: "Negro families with better than average educational levels do, in general, succeed in 'passing along' a comparable level of *educational* attainment to their children. But, again, the latter are less able than are white children to convert such attainment into occupational achievement and commensurate monetary returns to education."[5]

If we use the conditions described by Duncan in the late 1960s as our baseline, we have to conclude that the late twentieth and early twenty-first centuries have brought improvements in the educational and occupational attainments of middle-class blacks. We saw this from the statistics on education and occupation in chapters 6 and 7 and from the comparison of the thirty-one couples' educational achievement to that of their parents, few of whom had college degrees. Yet the success of the interviewees' generation was mixed. Not all siblings earned college degrees. However, given the efforts on behalf of their children's education that were described in chapter 9, it seems likely that their children will replicate their parents' successes in educational attainment. Still, the obstacles African Americans face in the attainment process are severe. As we saw in chapter 7, about half of the upper-middle-class men and women I interviewed had experienced workplace discrimination in income or promotion.

The twenty-first century has witnessed greater opportunities in residential choice; specifically, more middle-class blacks are moving into the suburbs. Nevertheless, black middle-class suburbanization is a mixed achievement. On the positive side, it marks an increase in their ability to move around the metropolis more freely in search of a residence, a right that was severely constrained until recently. Yet even this expansion of the right to choose their own residence is accompanied by limitations. As sociologist John Logan has noted, middle-class black suburbanites are more likely than white suburbanites to live in proximity to poverty areas. Then there is the finding of Myron Orfield and Thomas Luce that predominantly black suburban neighborhoods fare worse than integrated ones in economic resources and educational opportunities. Prince George's County, the largest and most affluent of middle-class suburbs, seems to support their finding. The thirty-one couples I interviewed struggle with both an underperforming educational system and the lack of upscale shopping and dining services like those available in neighboring predominantly white suburbs. It is true that Prince George's County is near the lower limit of the threshold Orfield and Luce use in their classification of "largely non-white residents": 60 percent or higher. The black percentage of the county, also, appears to be growing very slowly, from 64.5 percent in 2010 to 65 percent in 2016. Is this the reason for the recent growth in upscale services in the county? Or have the new services been the result of the efforts of an efficient political administration that has expended considerable time and money to attract the likes of Wegmans and Whole Foods supermarkets? The county does not yet have upscale "white tablecloth" restaurants, except for those in National Harbor and the MGM

Casino. Yet it appears that companies are beginning to recognize the opportunities that exist in this affluent black middle-class market. With improvements in the county's school system, Prince George's may yet become a predominantly minority suburban county that provides its residents with both upscale services and effective education for their children.

As we saw in earlier chapters, there is another dimension to black middle-class suburbanization besides the economy, services, and education. Rather than decry the lack of diversity in their communities, black middle-class families are seeking out neighborhoods that are predominantly or all black. This suggests that the growth of predominantly black upper-middle-class suburban communities is a trend that is likely to continue wherever possible. It seems that large percentages of upper-middle-class blacks are no longer concerned with integration. Most of the couples in my sample were emphatic in asserting their preference for living in black upper-middle-class communities. While they did not reject integration totally, it was clear that it was only welcome on their terms: whites moving in while black residents remain in power. This is a far-reaching development in the history of residential patterns and upends previous assumptions of the residential goals of middle-class blacks.

Are there broader lessons here for the new black middle class at large? In chapter 1, we learned that Prince George's County is one of eleven metros with the highest concentrations of suburban blacks. These eleven suburbs are also concentrations of the new black middle class. We can assume that the other ten face the same economic, service, and educational challenges as Prince George's County. In fact, these challenges are likely to be greater in the seven smaller southern suburbs because of fewer resources. Among the four largest black suburban concentrations (Atlanta, Dallas, Houston, and Washington, D.C.), DeKalb County, Georgia, in the Atlanta suburbs comes closest to Prince George's County because of the high concentration of historically black colleges and universities in Atlanta. In 2016, 55 percent of DeKalb County was African American, and of the 41 percent of county college graduates in 2010, 26 percent were black. The twenty-first century has indeed brought significant advances for the new black middle class in improved attainment and residential choice, yet many challenges remain. It remains to be seen whether predominantly black upper-middle-class suburbs can become communities with vibrant school systems, economic opportunities, and upscale services comparable to diverse and predominantly white middle-class suburbs.

Appendix

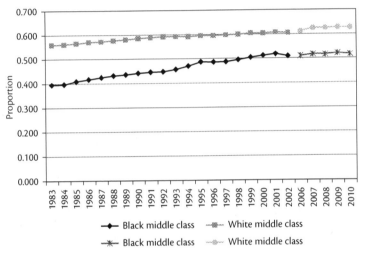

FIG. A.1. Total Middle Class by Race, 1983–2010
Source: See note 4 of the Introduction.

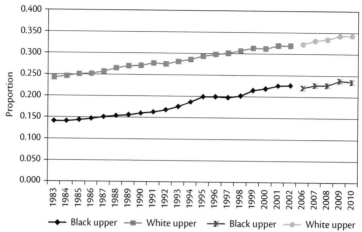

FIG. A.2. Upper Middle Class by Race, 1983–2010
Source: See note 4 of the Introduction.

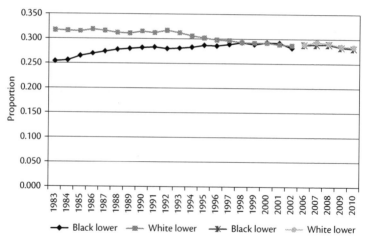

FIG. A.3. Lower Middle Class by Race, 1983–2010
Source: See note 4 of the Introduction.

Acknowledgments

Writing a book is seldom a solo endeavor. The outcome typically depends on the input of many generous individuals. I wish to first express my gratitude to the thirty-one couples who gave so generously of their time. Their willingness to spend two hours (sometimes more) discussing their lives with me amid the demands of work, family life, and childcare made this book possible. I have used pseudonyms throughout. Research grants from the Sloan and Spencer Foundations enabled me to employ graduate students whose skills I came to depend on. Kendra Barber, Aleia Clark, and Paul Dean, thank you for your help with the interviews. I hope it was also a learning experience for you in your development as sociologists. The time you spent transcribing and analyzing interviews using ATLAS.ti was also invaluable and hopefully contributed to your preparation for your own qualitative research. Two anonymous readers offered valuable comments that improved the content and presentation.

The support of my editor, Peter Mickulas, has made the process of finalizing the manuscript and the many prepublication details much easier to handle. I am grateful for his steady hand and patience. Finally, I want to thank my wife for her encouragement and support throughout the long process of writing this book.

Notes

Introduction

1. Bart Landry, *The New Black Middle Class* (Berkeley: University of California Press, 1987).
2. Max Weber, "The Distribution of Power within the Political Community: Class, Status, Party," in *Economy and Society*, vol. 2, trans. G. Roth and C. Wittich (Berkeley: University of California Press, 1978 [1921]), 926–940.
3. Karl Marx, *Capital*, vol. 1, *A Critique of Political Economy*, trans. Ben Fowkes (New York: Vintage, 1977 [1867]).
4. The data used to construct Figures A.1, A.2, and A.3 of the Appendix come from two different census occupational schemes. The first, for the years 1983 to 2002, is based on the Census Bureau's 1990 occupational classification, which was used until 2000. Beginning in 2000, a new occupational classification—incompatible with the earlier ones—was introduced. As a result, for the years 2006 to 2010 I turned to the new Integrated Public Use Microdata Series (IPUMS) based on the Census Bureau's 1990 occupational classification (Steven Ruggles, Katie Genadek, Ronald Goeken, Josiah Grover, and Matthew Sobek, Integrated Public Use Microdata Series: Version 7.0 [dataset]. Minneapolis: University of Minnesota, 2017, https://doi.org/10.18128/D010.V7.0). This resulted in a three-year gap in the data for the years 2003, 2004, and 2005. Class percentages are based on individuals in the *respective* labor forces of blacks and whites. These percentages of the noninstitutional civilian labor forces varied little in 2016: 62.3 percent of whites and 61.3 percent of blacks.

5. E. Franklin Frazier, *Black Bourgeoisie* (New York: Free Press, 1957).

6. Joe R. Feagin and Melvin P. Sikes, *Living with Racism: The Black Middle-Class Experience* (Boston: Beacon Press, 2006); Sharon Collins, *Black Corporate Executives: The Making and Breaking of a Black Middle Class* (Philadelphia: Temple University Press, 1997); Mary Pattillo-McCoy, *Black Picket Fences: Privilege and Peril among the Black Middle Class* (Chicago: University of Chicago Press, 1999); Karyn R. Lacy, *Blue-Chip Black: Race, Class, and Status in the New Black Middle Class* (Berkeley: University of California Press, 2007).

7. Bart Landry and Kris Marsh, "The Evolution of the New Black Middle Class," *Annual Review of Sociology* 37 (2011): 373–394.

8. See Dalton Conley, *Being Black, Living in the Red: Race, Wealth, and Social Policy in America* (Berkeley: University of California Press, 1999); Lisa A. Keister, *Wealth in America: Trends in Wealth Inequality* (New York: Cambridge University Press, 2000).

9. Andrew Wiese, *Places of Their Own: African American Suburbanization in the Twentieth Century* (Chicago: University of Chicago Press, 2004). See also Pattillo-McCoy, *Black Picket Fences*.

1. The New Black Middle Class and the Demographics of the Twenty-First Century

1. Andrew Wiese, *Places of Their Own: African American Suburbanization in the Twentieth Century* (Chicago: University of Chicago Press, 2004).

2. William H. Frey, *Melting Pot Cities and Suburbs: Racial and Ethnic Change in Metro America in the 2000s* (Washington, D.C.: Brookings Institution, 2011).

3. William H. Frey, *Diversity Explosion: How New Racial Demographics Are Remaking America* (Washington, D.C.: Brookings Institution Press, 2015).

4. Myron Orfield and Thomas Luce, "America's Racially Diverse Suburbs: Opportunities and Challenges," *Housing Policy Debate* 23, no. 2 (2013): 395–430.

5. Orfield and Luce, "America's Racially Diverse Suburbs," 2.

6. Orfield and Luce, "America's Racially Diverse Suburbs," 3.
7. John R. Logan, *Separate and Unequal in Suburbia*, Census Brief prepared for Project US2010, 2014, 6.
8. Logan, *Separate and Unequal in Suburbia*, 6.

2. Suburbanization of the New Black Middle Class

1. Ira Berlin, *Generations of Captivity: A History of African-American Slaves* (Cambridge, Mass.: Harvard University Press, 2003).
2. David J. Dent, "The New Black Suburbs," *New York Times Magazine*, July 12, 1992.

3. Changing Neighborhoods

1. Douglas S. Massey and Nancy A. Denton, *American Apartheid: Segregation and the Making of the Underclass* (Cambridge, Mass.: Harvard University Press, 1998).
2. Frank Parkin, *Marxism and Class Theory: A Bourgeois Critique* (New York: Columbia University Press, 1979).
3. Robert Novak, *The Rise of the Unmeltable Ethnics: The New Political Force of the Seventies* (New York: Macmillan, 1972).

4. Pick Up the Newspaper; We're Out of Town

1. Robert D. Putnam, *Bowling Alone: The Collapse and Revival of American Community* (New York: Simon and Schuster, 2000).

5. Catch-22

1. Lawrence Feinberg, "P.G. School, NAACP Leaders Agree to Curb Busing," *Washington Post*, February 28, 1979.
2. Jackson Diehl, "Board Shifts Policy in Move to Shut Down Schools in P.G.," *Washington Post*, February 12, 1979.
3. Feinberg, "P.G. School, NAACP Leaders."
4. Leon Wynter, "Busing Contradictions Cause Desegregation Paradox," *Washington Post*, July 2, 1983.

5. Wynter, "Busing Contradictions Cause Desegregation Paradox."
6. Wynter, "Busing Contradictions Cause Desegregation Paradox."
7. Wynter, "Busing Contradictions Cause Desegregation Paradox," 2.

6. Educating the New Black Middle Class

1. C. Wright Mills, *White Collar: The American Middle Classes* (New York: Oxford, 1951).
2. William H. Whyte, *The Organization Man* (New York: Simon and Schuster, 1956).
3. M. Hout, "Occupational Mobility of Black Men: 1962–1973," *American Sociological Review* 49 (2003): 308–322; R. A. Miech, W. Easton, and K. Liang, "Occupational Stratification over the Life Course: A Comparison of Occupational Trajectories across Race and Gender during the 1980s and 1990s," *Work and Occupations* 30 (2003): 440–473; K. Yamaguchi, "Black-White Differences in Social Mobility in the Past 30 Years: A Latent-Class Regression Analysis," *Research in Social Stratification and Mobility* 27 (2009): 65–78.
4. In "The Evolution of the New Black Middle Class," *Annual Review of Sociology* 37 (2011): 373–394, Kris Marsh and I review much of the literature on black mobility. See also Dalton Conley, *Being Black, Living in the Red: Race, Wealth, and Social Policy in America* (Berkeley: University of California Press, 1999). For an excellent study of the role of gender on Wall Street, see Louise Marie Roth, *Selling Women Short: Gender and Money on Wall Street* (Princeton, N.J.: Princeton University Press, 2006).
5. Pamela R. Bennett and Yu Xie, "Revisiting Racial Differences in College Attendance: The Role of Historically Black Colleges and Universities," *American Sociological Review* 68 (August 2003): 573.
6. Thomas J. Kane, "College Entry by Blacks since 1970: The Role of College Costs, Family Background, and the Returns to Education," *Journal of Political Economy* 102, no. 5 (October 1994): 878–911.
7. See Appendix A.
8. Pamela R. Bennett and Yu Xie, "Revisiting Racial Differences in College Attendance," 579. Italics in original.

9. Mikyong Minsun Kim and Clifton F. Conrad, "The Impact of Historically Black Colleges and Universities on the Academic Success of African-American Students," *Research in Higher Education* 47, no. 4 (June 2006): 399–427.

10. Walter R. Allen, "The Color of Success: African-American College Student Outcomes at Predominantly White and Historically Black Public Colleges and Universities," *Harvard Educational Review* 62, no. 1 (February 1992): 26–44.

7. From School to Work

1. I use the IPUMS-USA data in this comparison for the years 1970, 1980, 1990, and 2000. Using this index is not without problems, especially when making comparisons over time. Variations in the number of occupational titles over time may increase or decrease the index. The problem is addressed in these comparisons by adopting the standardized occupation scheme developed by IPUMS-USA using the 1990 U.S. Census occupational classification.

2. The 1980 and 1990 occupational statistics are based on the decennial censuses, while the 2000 to 2002 occupational statistics were compiled by IPUMS-USA from Current Population Survey (CPS) data.

3. See Bart Landry and Kris Marsh, "The Evolution of the New Black Middle Class, *Annual Review of Sociology* 37 (2011): 373–394.

8. Income and Wealth

1. Census data for income by occupation come from the March supplement of the Current Population Survey (CPS), now called the Annual Social and Economic Supplement. It is limited by the sample size and does not show income for all occupations. Nevertheless, it is very useful for making meaningful comparisons across groups.

2. Meizhu Lui, Barbara Robles, Betsy Leondar-Wright, Rose Brewer, and Rebecca Adamson, *The Color of Wealth: The Story behind the U.S. Racial Wealth Divide* (New York: New Press, 2006); Melvin L. Oliver and Thomas M. Shapiro, *Black Wealth/White Wealth: A New Perspective*

on Racial Inequality (New York: Routledge, 1995); Thomas M. Shapiro, *The Hidden Cost of Being African American: How Wealth Perpetuates Inequality* (New York: Oxford University Press, 2004).

3. Sharmila Choudhury, "Racial and Ethnic Differences in Wealth and Asset Choices," *Social Security Bulletin* 64, no. 4 (2001/2002).

Afterword

1. Petula Dvorak, "Often-Snubbed Pr. George's Scores the Grocery Holy Grail: Wegmans," *Washington Post*, October 22, 2010.
2. Quoted in Ovetta Wiggins, "New Prince George's Wegmans Becoming a Social Hot Spot," *Washington Post*, February 17, 2011.
3. Wiggins, "New Prince George's Wegmans."
4. Luz Lazo, "Whole Foods Debuts in Riverdale Park, Another Symbol of Prince George's Progress," *Washington Post*, April 11, 2017.
5. Maryland National Capital Park and Planning Commission, *Selected Demographic and Economic Data for Prince George's County, Maryland*, prepared by the M-NCPPC, Research Section, 2010.
6. Kimbriell Kelly, John Sullivan, and Steven Rich, "Broken by the Bubble: In the Fairwood Subdivision, Dreams of Black Wealth Were Dashed by the Housing Crisis," *Washington Post*, January 25, 2015.

Conclusion

1. Otis Dudley Duncan, "Inheritance of Poverty or Inheritance of Race?," in Daniel P. Moynihan, ed., *On Understanding Poverty: Perspectives from the Social Sciences* (New York: Basic Books, 1968), 85–110.
2. Peter M. Blau, Otis Dudley Duncan, David L. Featherman, and Robert M. Hauser, *Occupational Changes in a Generation, 1962 and 1973* (Ann Arbor, MI: Inter-university Consortium for Political and Social Research), https://doi.org/10.3886/ICPSR06162.v1.
3. Duncan, "Inheritance of Poverty or Inheritance of Race?," 100.
4. Duncan, "Inheritance of Poverty or Inheritance of Race?," 102.
5. Duncan, "Inheritance of Poverty or Inheritance of Race?," 96. Emphasis in original.

Index

Page numbers in *italics* indicate figures and tables.

Civil Rights Act of 1964, 1, 128–129, 144, 158

class: in migration to Prince George's County, 26–30; occupation and, 2, 3–4, 91–93, 99, 152–153; school system and, 78; three-stage process of attainment of, 93; upward mobility, education, and, 90–94. *See also* lower middle class; middle class; upper middle class

classroom size, 189

climate of workplace, 148

college, choice of: for children, 193–196; in 1970s, 101–105; in 1980s, 107–111

college education: for children, 179–182; entrance process, 100; explanations for deficit in attainment of, 97–99; financing of, for children, 197–200; history of attainment of, 94–97; in 1990s, 117–120; percentage of African Americans and whites with, *95, 97*; on predominantly white campuses, 105–107, 112–115; preparation for, 191–193; residential location of graduates, 12–13. *See also* college, choice of; historically black colleges and universities

Collins, Sharon, *Black Corporate Executives*, 4, 132

Columbia, Maryland, 19

Columbia, South Carolina, metro area, 9, 13

community, formation of: acquaintances, friends, and, 61–63; exchange of services in, 63–65; friendliness, receptivity, and, 58–59; proximity and, 57–58; race and, 59–60; satisfaction with life and, 66–67; shared values and, 60–61; structural features of neighborhoods and, 65–66

control of institutions and class struggles, 44

cultural diversity, exposing children to, 52–56

Curry, Wayne, 47, 201

Dallas, Texas, metro area, 9, 11, 13

Deasy, John, 202

DeKalb County, Georgia, 212–213

demography: of Prince George's County, 18, 23–24, 38, 76–77, 164–165; of United States, 8–13

Dent, David, "The New Black Suburbs," 16, 17, 21

Denton, Nancy A., 42

desegregation: of colleges and universities, 94, 101; of school systems, 42–46, 76–78. *See also* integration; segregation

dining options, dissatisfaction with, 86–89

discrimination: experience of, 209; occupational attainment and, 122–123; in workplace, 144–151, 211. *See also* Civil Rights Act of 1964; segregation

dissatisfaction with Prince George's County: dining options, 86–89; overview, 68; school system, 70–74, 80–81, 189; shopping options, 70, 81–86

diverse residential patterns, 37–38, 89

diversity of suburbs, 7–10

Duncan, Otis Dudley, "Inheritance of Poverty or Inheritance of Race?," 209–210

economic downturn of 2008, 206–208

education: of children, importance of, 74–75; upward mobility and, 90–94. *See also* educational attainment; school system

educational attainment: black middle-class suburbs and, 12–13; improvements in, 210–211; of parents, and college attainment of children, 98. *See also* college education

employment. *See* labor force entry; occupational attainment

enrichment activities for children, 186–189

Orfield, Myron, 10, 37–38, 89, 211
The Organization Man (Whyte), 92
ownership of property and class
    membership, 2. *See also* home
    ownership

parental involvement in education,
    182–186, 189–190
Parkin, Frank, 44
Pattillo-McCoy, Mary, 4
pension accounts, 161, 175
personal use, wealth for, 153
place, search for, 7. *See also* residential
    location
Places of Their Own (Wiese), 7
poverty: intergenerational, 209–210;
    proximity of black suburbs to areas
    of, 211; research on, 3; in South-
    east D.C., 25; in suburbs, 9–11
Prince George's County, Maryland:
    demography of, 18, 23–24, 38, 76–77,
    164–165; description of, 11–12, 15;
    desegregation in, 45–46, 76–78;
    foreclosures in, 206–208; history of,
    16–17; "inside the beltway," 25, 76, 77,
    78; malls in, 82; "middle ring" of, 77–78;
    political changes in, 47, 201–202;
    white flight from, 38–42, 76. *See also*
    dissatisfaction with Prince George's
    County; migration to Prince George's
    County; school system; *specific cities*
Prince George's Plaza, 82
productive wealth, 153
professionals: income of, and race,
    157–158; percentage of black and white
    female, *124, 127*; percentage of black
    and white male, *125, 126*. *See also*
    occupational attainment
promotions, being passed over for,
    146–148
property ownership: class membership
    and, 2; home ownership, 153, 160, 162,
    164–169, 206–208; investment
    property, 169–175
proximity in community formation, 57–58

public compared to private schools, 76,
    79–81, 189–190
public compared to private sector
    occupations, 126–127, 130
Putnam, Robert D., 57

quintiles, income, 154, *155*

race: access to college education and,
    97–99; being first and, 133–135;
    college attainment and, 94–97, *95, 97*;
    college experience and, 105–106; in
    formation of community, 59–60;
    income distribution by, 155–158, *156,
    157*; intergenerational poverty and,
    209–210; of mentors, 144; middle
    class by, *215*; in migration to Prince
    George's County, 30–33; occupational
    titles ranked by, 123–128, *124–125*;
    upper and lower middle classes by,
    216; upscale shopping options and,
    84; wealth and, 159–164
Radford University, 107–108, 113
recruitment of black students, 101–102
"redlining," 8
residential integration, 47–56, 212
residential location: choice of, 14;
    housing wealth and, 168–169; as
    mixed achievement, 211–212;
    navigation of, 6; suburbs, 7–13
retirement accounts, 161–162, 163,
    175–177
Richmond, Virginia, metro area, 9, 13
role models, professional, 33–36

salary discrimination, 148
scholarships, 109–111, 199
school system: choice of public or private,
    189–190; desegregation of, 42–46,
    76–78; dissatisfaction with, 70–74,
    80–81, 189; financial status of, 202–204;
    history of, 75–79; magnet schools, 79,
    190–191; parental involvement in,
    182–186, 189–190; quality of schools
    in, 79–81, 191; restructuring of, 202

segregation: in Maryland, 16; of
neighborhoods, 38–42; occupational
attainment and, 122–123; in Prince
George's County, 17; of schools, 76;
in suburbs, 10. *See also* desegregation
shopping options, 70, 81–86, 204–205
Sikes, Melvin P., 4
slavery in Maryland, 15–16
Social Security, 161–162
socioeconomic conditions: college
attainment and, 97–99; college choice
and, 111. *See also* income; poverty
"some college," black adults with, 96, 99
southern metropolitan cities, suburban
black populations of, 8–9
southern states, migration from, 12
"spillover" suburbanization, 9, 25
standard of living, 2, 6, 151, 152–153
"stepping up," as motivation for
migration, 25–26, 29
stereotypes, confronting, 3, 107, 134–135
stock ownership, 153, 160–161, 162–163,
169, 172–175
structural features of neighborhoods,
65–66
subprime mortgage loans, 207–208
suburban communities, movement to,
7–13, 14–15. *See also* migration to
Prince George's County
summer academic programs, 186–187,
191–192

tangible assets, 159
Thornton, Alvin, 79
time required to enter labor force,
135–138
TRIM (Tax Reform Initiative by
residents of Prince George's County),
203
tuition costs, 197
Tuskegee University, 104

University of Maryland, 102–103, 106
upper class, 2, 159–160
upper middle class: division between
lower middle class and, 92–93; home
ownership in, 166; occupations and,
122, 123; professions of, 2, 5; by race,
216
upward mobility and education,
90–94

values, shared, in community
formation, 60–61
Virginia Tech, 108, 112–113

Washington, D.C.: Southeast, 25;
suburban black population of, 9, 11,
12–13, 14–15
wealth: black compared to white,
159–164; home ownership and, 160,
162, 164–169; retirement accounts
and, 175–177; standard of living and,
153; stocks, investment property, and,
169–175. *See also* income
Weber, Max, 2, 91, 92, 121, 152
Wegmans supermarket, 204–205
White Collar (Mills), 92
white-collar middle class, 2, 91–92
whites: movement from Prince George's
County by, 38–42, 76; movement to
suburbs by, 7–8; share of aggregate
group income of, *156*
Whole Foods, 205
Whyte, William H., *The Organization
Man*, 92
Wiese, Andrew, *Places of Their
Own*, 7
Woodmore Towne Centre, 205
working class, 2, 91–92
workplace: discrimination in, 144–151,
211; mentorship in, 140–144
Wynter, Lynn, 79

About the Author

BART LANDRY received his PhD in sociology from Columbia University and has spent the better part of his career studying class inequality. This has included research at the intersections of class and family, class and technology workers, and class and race. His major publications include *The New Black Middle Class* and *Black Working Wives: Pioneers of the American Family Revolution.* He is a professor emeritus of sociology at the University of Maryland, College Park.